'ALLO 'ALLO 2
'The Camembert Caper'

Based on the original
BBC TV series written by
Jeremy Lloyd and David Croft

Adapted by David Pibworth,
David Lovesy, and Steve Clark

Copyright © 2023 by Jeremy Lloyd and David Croft
Adaptation © 2023 David Pibworth, David Lovesy, and Steve Clark
All Rights Reserved

'ALLO 'ALLO 2 'THE CAMEMBERT CAPER' is fully protected under the copyright laws of the British Commonwealth, including Canada, the United States of America, and all other countries of the Copyright Union. All rights, including professional and amateur stage productions, recitation, lecturing, public reading, motion picture, radio broadcasting, television, online/digital production, and the rights of translation into foreign languages are strictly reserved.

ISBN 978-0-573-00032-4

concordtheatricals.co.uk
concordtheatricals.com

FOR PRODUCTION ENQUIRIES

UNITED KINGDOM AND WORLD
EXCLUDING NORTH AMERICA
licensing@concordtheatricals.co.uk

020-7054-7298

NORTH AMERICA
info@concordtheatricals.com
1-866-979-0447

Each title is subject to availability from Concord Theatricals, depending upon country of performance.

CAUTION: Professional and amateur producers are hereby warned that *'ALLO 'ALLO 2 'THE CAMEMBERT CAPER'* is subject to a licensing fee. The purchase, renting, lending or use of this book does not constitute a licence to perform this title(s), which licence must be obtained from the appropriate agent prior to any performance. Performance of this title(s) without a licence is a violation of copyright law and may subject the producer and/or presenter of such performances to penalties. Both amateurs and professionals considering a production are strongly advised to apply to the appropriate agent before starting rehearsals, advertising, or booking a theatre. A licensing fee must be paid whether the title is presented for charity or gain and whether or not admission is charged.

This work is published by Samuel French, an imprint of Concord Theatricals Ltd.

The Professional Rights in this play are controlled by Worldwide Theatrix Ltd, 105 Risbygate Street, Bury St Edmunds, IP33 3AA.

No one shall make any changes in this title for the purpose of production. No part of this book may be reproduced, stored in a retrieval system, scanned, uploaded, or transmitted in any form, by any means, now known or yet to be invented, including mechanical, electronic, digital, photocopying, recording, videotaping, or otherwise, without the prior written permission of the publisher. No one shall share this title, or part of this title, to any social media or file hosting websites.

The moral right of Jeremy Lloyd, David Croft, David Pibworth, David Lovesy, and Steve Clark to be identified as author of this work has been asserted in accordance with Section 77 of the Copyright, Designs and Patents Act 1988.

USE OF COPYRIGHTED MUSIC

A licence issued by Concord Theatricals to perform this play does not include permission to use the incidental music specified in this publication. In the United Kingdom: Where the place of performance is already licensed by the PERFORMING RIGHT SOCIETY (PRS) a return of the music used must be made to them. If the place of performance is not so licensed then application should be made to PRS for Music (www.prsformusic.com). A separate and additional licence from PHONOGRAPHIC PERFORMANCE LTD (www.ppluk.com) may be needed whenever commercial recordings are used. Outside the United Kingdom: Please contact the appropriate music licensing authority in your territory for the rights to any incidental music.

USE OF COPYRIGHTED THIRD-PARTY MATERIALS

Licensees are solely responsible for obtaining formal written permission from copyright owners to use copyrighted third-party materials (e.g., artworks, logos) in the performance of this play and are strongly cautioned to do so. If no such permission is obtained by the licensee, then the licensee must use only original materials that the licensee owns and controls. Licensees are solely responsible and liable for clearances of all third-party copyrighted materials, and shall indemnify the copyright owners of the play(s) and their licensing agent, Concord Theatricals Ltd., against any costs, expenses, losses and liabilities arising from the use of such copyrighted third-party materials by licensees.

IMPORTANT BILLING AND CREDIT REQUIREMENTS

If you have obtained performance rights to this title, please refer to your licensing agreement for important billing and credit requirements.

'ALLO 'ALLO 2 'THE CAMEMBERT CAPER' was first performed by Milton Keynes Theatre of Comedy at the Chrysalis Theatre, Milton Keynes in September 2013 with kind permission by David Croft. Directed by David Pibworth. The cast was as follows:

THE FRENCH

RENÉ ARTOIS ....David Lovesy
EDITH ....Sue Whyte
YVETTE..Melanie Best
MIMI ....Michelle Johnson
MICHELLE OF THE RESISTANCE...................... Vicky Amies
MONSIEUR ALPHONSE ....Gary Martindale
MONSIEUR LECLERC ....Jon Davis
MADAME FANNY...................................Erika Benning

THE GERMANS

COLONEL VON STROHM .... Richard Duncombe
LT. GRUBER ....Chris Tennant
CAPT. GEERING .... Alex Taylor
HERR FLICK...................................... Sean McDermott
HELGA.. Tracy Butler
GENERAL VON KLINKERHOFFEN...................Matthew Perris

THE BRITISH

OFFICER CRABTREE .... Steve Clark
BRITISH AIRMEN ....Keith Lennox and Neil Harrison

ENSEMBLE............. Roger Widdecombe, Jen Barber, Emma Dell, Matt Bayfield, Sandra Cowling, John Hopkins

CHARACTERS

THE FRENCH

RENÉ ARTOIS – Male, our hero. A café owner in war-torn France
EDITH ARTOIS – Female, René's wife
MONSIEUR ALPHONSE – Male, an elderly but wealthy funeral director
MADAM FANNY LA FAN – Female, the bed-ridden, elderly mother of Edith
YVETTE CARTE-BLANCHE – Female, a waitress
MIMI LABONQ – Female, another (shorter) waitress
MICHELLE DUBOIS – Female, an agent for the French Resistance
MONSIEUR LECLERC – Male, the Resistance's forger and master of disguise

THE GERMANS

GENERAL VON KLINKERHOFFEN – Male, the ruthless commander of the district
COLONEL VON STROHM – Male, Commandant of the town of Nouvien
CAPTAIN GEERING – Male, aide to the Colonel
LIEUTENANT GRUBER – Male, a (camp) German tank officer
HERR FLICK – Male, head of the local Gestapo
PRIVATE HELGA – Female, secretary to the Colonel and lover of Herr Flick

THE BRITISH

OFFICER CRABTREE – Male, a British agent (disguised as a Policeman)
FLIGHT LIEUTENANT FAIRFAX – Male, a British airman requiring repatriation
FLIGHT LIEUTENANT CARSTAIRS – Male, a second British airman
RADIO VOICE – Male/Female, the voice of SOE in London.
RADIO VOICE #2 – Male/Female, a second radio voice. Johnson's tailors in Wimbledon.

THE ENSEMBLE

SUPPORTING CHORUS – Male/Female
GERMAN SOLDIERS, MEMBERS OF THE RESISTANCE AND ASSORTED FRENCH PEASANTS

SETTING

The action of the play takes place in and around Café René in Occupied France, World War Two.

ACT ONE

Scene One – René's Café
René, French Peasants, Airmen, Yvette, Crabtree, Michelle, Mimi, Edith, Alphonse

Scene Two – The Colonel's HQ
Colonel, Geering, Gruber, Helga, General

Scene Three – Fanny's Bedroom
Fanny, Edith, René, Mimi, Michelle, Crabtree, Airmen, Radio Voice

Scene Three – Herr Flicks' Dungeon
Flick, Helga

Scene Five – René's Café
René, French Peasants, Mimi, Yvette, Colonel, Geering, Gruber, Edith, Leclerc, Michelle

Scene Six – The Funeral Parlour
Edith, René, Alphonse

Scene Seven – René's Café
René, French Peasants, German Soldiers, Yvette, Mimi, Edith, Colonel, Gruber, Geering, General, Crabtree, Michelle, Flick, Helga, Airmen, Leclerc

ACT TWO

Scene One – René's Café
René, Airmen, Michelle, Crabtree, Mimi, Alphonse, Yvette, Edith, Leclerc

Scene Two – The Colonel's HQ
Colonel, Geering, Gruber

Scene Three – The Railway Station
René, Yvette, Edith, Michelle, Crabtree, Airmen, Leclerc

Scene Four – Herr Flicks' Dungeon
Flick, Helga

Scene Five – The Château
General, Yvette, Helga, Flick, Gruber, René

Scene Six – Fanny's Bedroom
Fanny, René, Edith, Michelle, Crabtree, Leclerc, Radio Voice, Radio Voice 2, Mimi, Gruber

Scene Seven – René's Café
René, Yvette, Mimi, French Peasants, Colonel, Geering, Michelle, Flick, Helga, Edith, Gruber, General, German Soldiers, Fanny, Alphonse, Leclerc, Crabtree, Airmen

ACT ONE

Scene One
René's Café

(Sound effects: "'Allo, 'Allo" theme music*. Lights up on the café which is open for business. The café has a main door to the town square [with a bell that rings on entry], a door/exit leading to the back room/kitchen and a staircase leading upstairs. There is a bar area and a number of tables and chairs. **RENÉ** *is polishing glasses behind the bar. On a table at the back of the room are four French peasants, two male and two 'female' (they are actually the British airmen in disguise). The 'females' have their backs to the audience.* **RENÉ** *addresses the audience.)*

RENÉ. Ah, I was wondering when you might show up again at the Café René. I bid you welcome, of course, I don't know if you've eaten already but the pâté is particularly good – the camembert however is 'orribly

---

* A licence to produce *'Allo 'Allo 2* does not include a performance licence for "'Allo 'Allo theme music". The publisher and author suggest that the licensee contact PRS to ascertain the music publisher and contact such music publisher to license or acquire permission for performance of the song. If a licence or permission is unattainable for "'Allo 'Allo theme music", the licensee may not use the song in *'Allo 'Allo 2* but should create an original composition in a similar style or use a similar song in the public domain. For further information, please see the Music and Third-Party Materials Use Note on page iii.

warm and runny but I've got a lot to get rid of, so it is of course the 'Dish of the Day'. So why is my cheese so warm? Well, it's because my pantry is also hiding the two escaped British airmen who have not been able to get back to England. If you were party to our earlier adventures, you will remember that we ended the whole escapade with Edith and I as the proud owners of the masterpiece the 'The Fallen Madonna With The Big Boobies' by that master knocker painter Van Klomp. It is now stored in a safe place – sadly it is a *very* safe place because there were so many forgeries made of it no-one is really sure who has the real one anymore.

> *(During this speech, **YVETTE** has entered from the back room, and collected empty glasses from the peasant's table. **YVETTE** approaches **RENÉ** at the bar.)*

YVETTE. *(Seductively.)* Oh René, Madame Edith will be at the market for a little while yet, René, how about we pop in the pantry for a private party?

RENÉ. The café is open, Yvette. I have a business to run.

YVETTE. Oh, my love, how long is it?

RENÉ. *(Puzzled.)* Perhaps less than it was, but the stresses of war do not make it easy.

YVETTE. I mean how long is it since we last spent time alone together? I yearn to feel your powerful embrace once more.

RENÉ. Perhaps later, my sweet. When the café is closed, I might manage a hug on the rug in the snug.

YVETTE. Then later, my Gallic hero. (**YVETTE** *moves away and continues to tidy.)*

RENÉ. *(To audience.)* My wife Edith still does not suspect that I am having dalliances with my waitress Yvette…

and my other waitress Mimi...there is much going on for a businessman such as myself.

> (**YVETTE** *blows* **RENÉ** *a kiss as she leaves through the back door.*)

Luckily, I am prepared to put in the overtime.

> (**RENÉ** *makes to follow* **YVETTE** *offstage but is interrupted by the two peasant 'females' pushing their chairs back and standing up in indignation. The two males then stand up and make suggestive actions, and the 'females' both slap the male peasants who leave through the main door.*)

What is going on here?

> (*The two females turn to reveal they are in fact the* **BRITISH AIRMEN**, **FAIRFAX** *and* **CARSTAIRS** *in disguise.*)

FAIRFAX. I'm not sure what they were suggesting but I certainly haven't done anything like that since Harrow!

CARSTAIRS. Didn't sound like cricket at all, old boy.

RENÉ. (*Unable to understand any of this.*) What are you two idiots doing out here? You're supposed to be hiding in the pantry! What if the Germans were to walk in?

FAIRFAX. What's he saying?

CARSTAIRS. Haven't a clue old boy!

> (**MICHELLE** *enters with* **CRABTREE** *through the main door.* **RENÉ** *jumps at the ringing of the bell.*)

CRABTREE. Good moaning.

RENÉ. Oh my God! I thought that we'd had it then!

FAIRFAX. Carstairs! It's those resistance chappies!

CARSTAIRS. Thank heavens. I thought we'd be hiding in those cheeses forever.

RENÉ. What are you doing here Michelle? And why have you brought this foolish British agent who thinks he can speak French?

CRABTREE. *(To* **RENÉ**.*)* Are we a loon? We need to tick with you.

RENÉ. I am as a loon as I can be. What do you want? I have a business to run.

MICHELLE. Listen very carefully, I will say this only once… *(To the* **BRITISH AIRMEN**, *in British accent.)* Hello, chaps. Sorry about the delay, but good news! We've got a plan to get you back to Blighty!

RENÉ. Don't just stand there talking English in the middle of wartime France. Go out the back to do your plotting. It's not like I can understand a word you are saying.

> (**MICHELLE** *bundles the two* **BRITISH AIRMEN** *offstage through the back door, leaving* **RENÉ** *and* **CRABTREE** *alone.)*

CRABTREE. We have a plin to sand away the earmen.

RENÉ. Oh, well I understand that much better. *(To audience.)* He has a plan to send away the airmen.

CRABTREE. They will floo back home in a hat ear balloon.

RENÉ. A hot air balloon? Wherever did you get such a thing?

CRABTREE. We mode win ourselves. We have the biscuit already.

RENÉ. You 'ave the basket – but what about the balloon?

CRABTREE. We nood some thongs first. We will be in torch shitly.

RENÉ. I see. Well, flying the airmen out in a giant balloon floating over Nouvien shouldn't attract much attention.

CRABTREE. I do not know what you moan.

(**MICHELLE** *enters again from the back room.*)

MICHELLE. *(To* **CRABTREE**.*)* Have you explained the plan to René?

RENÉ. In his own inimitable way. Look, Michelle, I will help the Resistance where I can, unless of course it puts me in physical danger or costs me anything, but why do you insist on using this incompetent British agent?

MICHELLE. In my fight for the freedom of France, I will use any weapons that I can. Officer Crabtee has been a great help ever since he first arrived here in Nouvien.

CRABTREE. *(Reminiscing about his arrival in France.)* Ah yes, I remember it well. It was a dick night, and there was no min.

RENÉ. *(To audience.)* Dark night, no moon.

CRABTREE. I jumped out of a British bummer, which was being chased by some German farters. Now I am disgeezed as a polocemen so I am able to mauve about with complete frodom.

RENÉ. Good. Feel completely free to leave and take this fanatical female with you.

MICHELLE. René, listen very carefully, I shall say this only once.

RENÉ. What now?

MICHELLE. We will be back here shortly with a list of items we will need for our hot air balloon. You will find these items for us.

RENÉ. And if I don't?

MICHELLE. When the English pilots escape in the balloon, we will use your cowardly corpse for ballast. Come, Crabtree, we must escape like phantoms into the night.

CRABTREE. Forwool René. We will be bick looter.

> (**MICHELLE** and **CRABTREE** *exit through the main door.*)

RENÉ. *(To audience.)* And there goes my quiet life again. All I want is a little peace.

> (**MIMI** *enters down the stairs. She poses flirtatiously on the bottom step.*)

And here she is. Still, whilst no-one else is around… come to me, Mimi!

MIMI. Oh, René!

RENÉ. *(He embraces her.)* Oh, Mimi. *(Stops.)* I thought you had gone into town with Edith?

MIMI. She sent me back early to make the soup. She is still taking tea with Monsieur Alphonse.

RENÉ. Monsieur Alphonse? She sits drinking tea with another man whilst I toil to keep this cafe open. How unfaithful of her. Now, where were we? Ah, Mimi!

MIMI. *(Embracing him again.)* René, when will I ever get over you?

RENÉ. Well, Thursday's are good for me…

MIMI. I cannot hear your heart.

RENÉ. That is because you are listening to my appendix.

MIMI. Will you see me later?

RENÉ. How about you meet me in the coal cellar after dinner.

MIMI. The coal cellar? But I get so dirty in there!

RENÉ. *(Suggestively.)* I know.

MIMI. Naughty boy. And now I will go and make the soup for the diners tonight. Have you a favourite?

RENÉ. Cockaleekie?

> (**MIMI** *titters and exits up the stairs.*)

(To audience.) One dangerous job and two intimate meetings. Ah well, you have to take the rough with the smooth.

> (**EDITH** *enters through the front door with* **MONSIEUR ALPHONSE**. **ALPHONSE** *carries Edith's bag of grocery shopping.*)

Ah, my wife Edith. Things just got a lot rougher!

EDITH. Monsieur Alphonse, you are so gallant. You really did not 'ave to walk me home.

ALPHONSE. Nonsense, Madame Edith. I would not rest until I was certain you had returned unharmed. The streets are not safe for a beautiful woman such as yourself to traverse unaccompanied.

EDITH. You flatter me, Monsieur Alphonse. *(To* **RENÉ**.*)* René! Why do you never lavish me with such honeyed words?

RENÉ. I have been stung too often. And who are you, Monsieur, to make such overtures to my wife?

ALPHONSE. I, sir, am Monsieur Alphonse the undertaker. Madame Edith and I were discussing local affairs, we were chatting about this and that, you know how it is.

RENÉ. This and that?

ALPHONSE. *Mostly* that. But it was getting late and I walked her home to ensure she arrived home un-ravaged... *(With pointed contempt)* as any dutiful husband would do.

RENÉ. I have made sure she has stayed un-ravaged for many years, I can assure you of that.

EDITH. *(Sadly.)* It is true.

ALPHONSE. Until we meet again, Madame Edith.

> (**ALPHONSE** *kisses* **EDITH**'s *hand and exits through the main door.)*

RENÉ. Well, I can only hope you have had a lovely afternoon whilst I've been trying to run a business! Since you left, I have had the airmen running loose and the Resistance have threatened my life if I don't help with some new hare-brained scheme.

EDITH. And have you taken lunch up to my mother?

RENÉ. I did not realise it was on my 'to do' list. I had no idea she ate. I assumed she just lived out of spite. *(To audience.)* Edith's mother is bed-bound in the attic room. We are not the best of friends. Frankly, I have a better relationship with the Gestapo.

EDITH. You lazy, feckless fool! My mother cries out for sustenance and you cannot even fetch her the simplest of meals. Come upstairs with me. Even now we are due to receive a message from British Intelligence so we can check on mamma at the same time.

RENÉ. *(To audience.)* For reasons best known to themselves, the Resistance have built a wireless set into my mother-in-law's bed. Ah well, let us go and see how many other ways I can lay down my life in the name of France.

> (**EDITH** *and* **RENÉ** *exit up the stairs. Blackout.)*

Scene Two
The Colonel's HQ

(That same day. The **COLONEL**'s *office. There is a desk with chair, and two further chairs in front. There is a single door/entrance. There is a military-style map on one wall. The* **COLONEL** *appears to be hard at work reading a report in a manila folder with mounting interest, and then drops the folder to reveal he is reading a copy of a risqué magazine; 'Reichstag and Reichhens'. There is a knock at the door and the* **COLONEL** *hurriedly hides the magazine under his papers on his desk.)*

COLONEL. Enter!

*(***CAPTAIN GEERING*** and* **LIEUTENANT GRUBER** *enter.)*

Ah, Captain Geering, Lieutenant Gruber, come in.

GEERING. You sent for us Herr Colonel?

COLONEL. General Von Klinkerhoffen has returned to Nouvien and I understand he is not in a good mood.

GRUBER. Why is that Herr Colonel?

COLONEL. Because Gruber, he has no doubt heard all about the loss of the painting of 'The Fallen Madonna With The Big Boobies'…

GEERING. Yes, he wanted to get his hands on those boobies.

GRUBER. I never saw the appeal myself!

COLONEL. It is a great shame that the painting has disappeared.

GEERING. It was our retirement fund.

COLONEL. *Our* retirement fund Geering? *I* found it!

GEERING. Yes. But *we* know about it.

COLONEL. I suggest we just say nothing and try and keep a low profile until he has forgotten about it all.

>   (**HELGA** *enters.*)

What is it Helga?

HELGA. *(Shouting.)* General Von Klinkerhoffen!

>   (**GENERAL VON KLINKERHOFFEN** *enters. The other officers jump to attention.*)

GENERAL. Heil Hitler!

COLONEL. Heil Hitler!

HELGA. Heil Hitler!

GRUBER. Heil Hitler!

GEERING. *(Late.)* 'Tler!

COLONEL. Ah, General, to what do we owe this pleasure?

GENERAL. I understand that we have lost the priceless painting of 'The Fallen Madonna With The Big Boobies' and it is all your fault!

GEERING. It's all our fault?

GENERAL. Ah, so you admit it. I had planned to sell it to fund a life of luxury after the war.

COLONEL. I'm sorry to hear that General, but it was nothing to do with us.

GENERAL. Nonsense. You will pay for your incompetence. To make it up, you must pay me fifty thousand francs by the end of the week, or you will all be sent to the Eastern Front.

COLONEL. Where are we going to find fifty thousand francs?

GENERAL. That is not my problem…it is *your* problem. If you cannot pay then you must find someone else who can.

GEERING. In Nouvien?

GENERAL. You have been too soft with these peasants. This is an occupation not a holiday. I have received word from Berlin that the Führer plans to reinforce this district in case of invasion. *(He indicates with a wooden pointer on the map on the wall.)* In this area we are deploying a regiment of artillery. In one month there will be over two thousand men camping here.

COLONEL. *(To **GRUBER**.)* Make a note of that, Gruber…

GRUBER. I already have.

GENERAL. Now get me that money. You have until Saturday night. Heil Hitler!

ALL. Heil Hitler!

GEERING. *(Late again.)* 'Tler!

*(The **GENERAL** exits.)*

COLONEL. What are we going to do? You heard the General. I don't want to end up on the Eastern Front.

GEERING. I have heard that the weather is terrible. The troops are forced to huddle together at night to keep warm.

GRUBER. That doesn't sound *too* terrible.

HELGA. I have a suggestion, Herr Colonel. We could insist that René in the café finds the money for us, after all, we know he has connections with the Resistance.

GEERING. Good idea.

GRUBER. But what if René refuses to help?

COLONEL. Simple. We say that we will tell the General that René is hiding the British airmen. And Helga, not a word of this to Herr Flick of the Gestapo.

HELGA. Of course not, Herr Colonel, although if he chooses to interrogate me, I may be forced to reveal it. He can be very persuasive.

COLONEL. You will just have to resist him. Geering, Gruber and I will visit René in his cafe...

GRUBER. I'm not too sure about this Colonel and I am very busy today...

COLONEL. ...Where we shall probe him. Yes, we shall pump him dry...

GRUBER. ...Although there's nothing that can't wait...

COLONEL. ...Of any money that he may have.

GRUBER. *(Slightly disappointed.)* Yes...yes...of course.

(Blackout.)

Scene Three
Fanny's Bedroom

(Later the same day. Lights up in Fanny's bedroom. There is a large bed with an iron bedframe, a bedside table, a window and a single door/entrance. **FANNY** *is in the bed with her ear trumpet. Unseen by the audience, the British airmen are hidden under/behind the bed.)*

FANNY. Edith! Edith! Oooh, I am so ill!

*(***FANNY*** realises no-one is listening and leans over and picks up her knitting from the side table. She starts knitting furiously, muttering.* **RENÉ** *and* **EDITH** *enter.* **EDITH** *carries a bowl of soup.)*

Edith, Edith, I am so ill and old...

RENÉ. Shut up and knit you old bat.

EDITH. Do not call my Mamma an old bat!

RENÉ. She *is* an old bat.

EDITH. That is not the point.

FANNY. What are you saying? I cannot hear.

RENÉ. Be quiet will you, we are awaiting an urgent message from London.

(The bed nobs light up. Sound Effects: Buzzing in time with the flashing!)

FANNY. Oh the knobs! The flashing knobs!

(This frightens **FANNY** *who screams and jumps at the noise and her knitting is thrown to the floor.)*

Oh my knitting, my stitching!

> (**FANNY** *leans over the bed to retrieve the knitting and lets out a fart. Sound effects: fart sound. She retrieves the knitting and holds it up in horror.*)

I've dropped one.

RENÉ. Oh dear me, yes you have.

EDITH. Get the radio, René.

RENÉ. I cannot lift the bed with my back. You lift it.

EDITH. I cannot lift the bed!

RENÉ. Where are those airmen when you need them?

> (*The* **BRITISH AIRMEN** *pop up from under/behind the bed wearing night dresses.*)

BRITISH AIRMEN. Hello!

RENÉ. Right you two, lift the bed up.

CARSTAIRS. What?

RENÉ. Lift the bed up.

FAIRFAX. What's he saying?

CARSTAIRS. No idea old boy.

RENÉ. Lift the bed up.

> (**RENÉ** *does it with actions showing them how to do it.*)

CARSTAIRS. Ah, morning exercises.

> (*The* **BRITISH AIRMEN** *both do some exercises.*)

FAIRFAX. Up down, up down.

RENÉ. What are you doing you silly people? Lift the bed up!

*(The **BRITISH AIRMEN** finally realise what **RENÉ** wants and lift up the bed. **FANNY** falls out with a thud.)*

EDITH. Be careful with Mamma. She is a weak and ill old lady.

*(**FANNY** pops up and clobbers **CARSTAIRS** with her ear trumpet and collapses back down again.)*

RENÉ. A weak and ill old lady when it suits her.

*(**RENÉ** takes the radio from under the bed and switches it on. Sound effects: Static and whistling.)*

RADIO. *(In a French accent.)* Nighthawk, Nighthawk, London calling. Are you receiving me? Over.

RENÉ. *(To **RADIO**.)* Yes, yes Nighthawk receiving London loud and not very clear. Over.

FANNY. Help me. Help me!

RENÉ. *(To **FANNY**.)* Shut up!

RADIO. I beg your pardon? Over.

RENÉ. *(To **RADIO**.)* Not you, sorry. I was talking to the mother-in-law. Over.

RADIO. Ah, right! Now please listen. Abandon the hot air balloon escape, I repeat abandon the hot air balloon escape. The airmen will be picked up at the airstrip north of the town tomorrow. Do you understand? Over.

RENÉ. *(To **RADIO**.)* Yes. Received and understood. Over.

RADIO. Good luck Nighthawk.

RENÉ. *(To **RADIO**.)* What with the escape or the mother-in-law?

RADIO. Both. Over and out.

> (**RENÉ** *puts the radio back under the bed and the* **BRITISH AIRMEN** *drop the bed.*)

FANNY. Help me back into bed.

EDITH. We will Mamma, we will.

> (**EDITH** *and the* **BRITISH AIRMEN** *help her back into bed.*)

FANNY. What is going on?

EDITH. Mamma, we are carrying out important work.

FANNY. I can't hear you. I can't hear him. I can't hear anything!

> (**RENÉ**, *fed up with* **FANNY**'s *shouting, looks around for the ear trumpet.* **MIMI** *enters just as* **RENÉ** *stands up with the ear trumpet.*)

RENÉ. I have the horn, I have the horn.

MIMI. Oh René!

> (**MIMI** *hugs* **RENÉ**. *He pushes her off with a worried glance to* **EDITH**, *and hands the trumpet to* **FANNY**.)

RENÉ. Get off. Get off. What do you want Mimi?

MIMI. Michelle of the Resistance is here to receive the message from London.

RENÉ. Oh, show her in.

> (**MICHELLE** *enters with* **CRABTREE**.)

MICHELLE. Have you the message?

RENÉ. Yes I have the message. The hot air balloon escape is abandoned.

CRABTREE. Oh, that is a sham. I have managed to get my hands on many pairs of knockers, bug and smell. I have had my hands full, I can tell you.

RENÉ. Knockers?

CRABTREE. Knockers. Knockers made of sulk.

MICHELLE. Why is the escape abandoned?

RENÉ. I am not privy to such information. I merely risk my life each day to pass on messages. All I know is that London told us to take the airmen to the airstrip north of the town tomorrow, which is very dangerous I might say.

MICHELLE. No, no, we will cunningly disguise them. What do we do once they are there?

RENÉ. I do not know. That is why it is all so dangerous.

CARSTAIRS. I think I heard the word dangerous in there somewhere. *(To* **CRABTREE.***)* What's dangerous?

CRABTREE. *(To the* **BRITISH AIRMEN** *in a British accent.)* There's been a change of plan. The hot air balloon is off!

FAIRFAX. Oh that's a shame. I've never been in a hot air balloon.

CRABTREE. *(To the* **BRITISH AIRMEN** *in a British accent.)* You are being taken to the airstrip, but you will have to wait a bit longer.

CARSTAIRS. Oh no. We really need to be going. If we stay much longer we may be caught by the Gestapo, and we don't want that.

FAIRFAX. No, we don't. We've known brave men who have shot themselves before that.

RENÉ. *(To* **CRABTREE.***)* What are they going on about now?

CRABTREE. They are seeing that they know brave men who have shat themselves.

RENÉ. Well I can't argue with that.

MICHELLE. René, hide them for another day. I will then return and disguise them and we will slip away.

RENÉ. Good.

CRABTREE. Well, I thonk it is time for us to pish off.

RENÉ. Just what I was thinking.

(Blackout.)

Scene Four
Herr Flick's Dungeon

(That evening. The Gestapo HQ. There is a desk and chair and a further chair in front, an assortment of torture equipment on the walls and a single entrance/door. **FLICK** *and* **HELGA** *are seated at the desk playing cards.* **HELGA***'s cards are down, but* **FLICK** *is still holding his cards. On the desk between them is a Gestapo pen and pencil set. There is also a telephone.)*

FLICK. How dare you try to bluff a senior Gestapo officer with a pair of tens? I have won. *(He puts his cards face down on the table.)*

HELGA. Am I allowed to see your hand, Herr Flick?

FLICK. No. You have lost. I get your Gestapo pen and pencil set. *(He grabs the set and slides it to his side of the desk.)*

HELGA. You have cleaned me out Herr Flick. If we play another round I will have nothing left to give you.

FLICK. Indeed.

HELGA. And I must admit it was not the activity I was expecting when you told me I should play my cards right.

FLICK. I needed the distraction. The British airmen, who are still hiding in Nouvien, are preying on my mind. If they are not caught soon I will be forced to send my Tracker badge back to the Hitler Youth.

HELGA. Then let me distract you further. General Von Klinkerhoffen is about to receive a large sum of money from the Colonel. It is my belief we may be able to take this money for ourselves.

FLICK. *Our*selves?

HELGA. *Your*self, of course, Herr Flick. Then we can run away together and make love on the beaches of the Caribbean.

FLICK. Quite impossible, Helga. The heat makes my leather coat too tight. But I can see us in a modest Alpine lodge overlooking the Matterhorn.

HELGA. Oh, Herr Flick, the thought of you as a lonely goatherd is driving me wild with desire. May I kiss you?

FLICK. You may. But just a quick one.

> *(They clinch.* **HELGA** *kisses him passionately. As ever, there is no response from* **HERR FLICK.***)*

That will do. This is a Gestapo office, not a bawdy house. Where is this money coming from?

HELGA. Colonel von Strohm is asking René at the Cafe René to raise it and then the Colonel will give it to the General to compensate him for the loss of 'The Fallen Madonna With The Big Boobies'.

FLICK. We also lost out on this painting. Helga. We will intercept this money ourselves. To that end, I will keep a watchful eye on René to see how he will produce this money.

HELGA. Perhaps it will come directly from selling his meals in the café.

FLICK. That would be a lot of knockwursts.

HELGA. I'm telling the truth, Herr Flick.

> *(Sound effects: Flick's phone rings.* **FLICK** *answers abruptly.)*

FLICK. Flick the Gestapo. *(Pause.)* No, I said Flick, the Gestapo. Clean out your ears, Von Smallhausen.

(Pause.) I see. I see. No, I will not be reporting that back to Head Office. I do not wish to look a right 'nana. *(He hangs up.)*

HELGA. Bad news?

FLICK. Gestapo business, Helga. But Von Smallhausen tells me that the British airmen may be in hiding near the Café René.

HELGA. You could watch for the money and keep an eye out for those airmen at the same time, Herr Flick.

FLICK. A double whammy. Very well. You have performed admirably, Helga. I will reward you.

HELGA. Thank you, Herr Flick.

FLICK. Your reward shall be an evening with me. I might take you to the movies.

HELGA. What is showing?

FLICK. Anything we want. I am Gestapo! Or we could stay here and amuse ourselves. I have a box of sharp needles somewhere.

>   *(**HERR FLICK** rifles through a drawer on the desk or takes them from his pocket. **HELGA** looks a little nervous.)*

(Finding them.) Ah, here they are.

HELGA. *(Worriedly.)* What have you in mind Herr Flick?

FLICK. I have an excellent gramophone, and many records of Hitler's speeches. They are quite amusing.

HELGA. *(Surprised.)* Hitler's speeches, quite amusing?

FLICK. Played at double speed, he sounds like Donald Duck.

>   *(Blackout.)*

Scene Five
René's Café

(The next day. The Café René. Peasants are sitting at the tables at the front, making chit-chat with the serving girls. **RENÉ** *and* **EDITH** *are behind the bar.)*

YVETTE. *(To the peasants.)* And can I get you anything else?

(A peasant whispers something in her ear.)

(Slapping him.) You naughty boy! *(Pause.)* Come back at eight o'clock. But the sugar tongs will cost you extra.

(The **COLONEL**, **GEERING** *and* **GRUBER** *enter and stand in the middle of the café.)*

COLONEL. Heil Hitler!

GEERING. *(Late.)* 'Tler!

RENÉ. Ah! Good afternoon, gentlemen. I trust you, and indeed Hitler, are all well? Where would you like to sit? We have several tables available.

COLONEL. You do. *(Indicating a table where the peasants are seated.)* We want this one.

RENÉ. Could I not press you to one with a better view? This one, for instance would put your back to my wife for your entire visit.

COLONEL. If you do not remove these peasants immediately, I will have them shot.

RENÉ. That seems a fairly extreme method of clearing a table.

COLONEL. Or, of course, I could have *you* shot.

RENÉ. Move over to this other table, peasant scum.

*(**RENÉ** hustles the peasants over to another table whilst **MIMI** and **YVETTE** bustle around the **GERMAN OFFICERS** as they take their seats. **YVETTE** is very friendly, but **MIMI** is far frostier with the **GERMANS**. **RENÉ** stays in the background placating the peasants.)*

YVETTE. Please take a seat. If there is anything that I can do for you, please let me know.

GEERING. *(Excitedly.)* Oh, we will, we will.

GRUBER. I'm fine, thank you.

COLONEL. Yvette, tell René that I must speak to him at once on urgent business.

YVETTE. At once, Colonel.

*(**EDITH** comes across to the Germans at the table. **YVETTE** goes across to **RENÉ**.)*

EDITH. You seem a little out-of-sorts today, Colonel.

COLONEL. I apologise, Madame Edith. The pressures of command weigh heavily on me. I have brought my two comrades to partake in wine and women.

EDITH. And song?

COLONEL. *(Quickly.)* No! Just wine and women...

GRUBER. Only wine for me.

EDITH. I have all sorts of songs in my repertoire whatever the occasion. I can sing something special no matter what fate throws at me.

RENÉ. *(Approaching from behind.)* Usually onions or stale bread rolls. You have something you wish to discuss, Colonel?

COLONEL. I do. René, times are not as they once were.

RENÉ. This I know. But I thought your war efforts were going your way?

GEERING. We should have them more often, you know. We do them so well.

COLONEL. Indeed, however, since the General thinks we lost his painting things have gotten very uncomfortable.

GRUBER. He is making it very hard for us.

RENÉ. I can imagine that is not a problem for you at least, Lieutenant.

COLONEL. I will be blunt. The General is demanding money from us to make up for the loss of the painting.

RENÉ. What? Well, I suppose we could have a whip round…

COLONEL. I could have everyone in the town roundly whipped, but it will not raise the money required. René, unless you get us fifty thousand francs I will have no choice but to drop you in it for hiding the British airmen.

RENÉ. But Colonel, I assure you they are long gone.

COLONEL. René, do not play me for a fool. Union Jack underpants have been seen drying on the line in your back yard more than once this past month.

RENÉ. Is that so? *(To himself.)* They will be drying at half-mast when I speak to them later. Colonel! Be reasonable! Where am I going to get fifty thousand francs?

GEERING. This is not our problem.

COLONEL. Hans is right. The how is not something I need to know – we just need the money. By Saturday night.

RENÉ. Saturday night? This is not possible. You might as well ask me to bring you the moon.

> *(**LECLERC** enters, in no disguise this time! **RENÉ** spots him and needs to get across to him.)*

Oh my God. Excuse me, Colonel, I must set plans in motion.

COLONEL. Saturday night, René. Or I'm afraid it's the firing squad for you.

> *(**RENÉ** hot foots it across to the bar, to speak with **LECLERC**.)*

RENÉ. And what do you want?

LECLERC. *(Raising his glasses.)* It is I, Leclerc!

RENÉ. I know! You're not even in disguise!

LECLERC. I am dressed as a sad, confused elderly man.

RENÉ. Need I say more? What can I do for you?

LECLERC. I bring a message from Michelle of the Resistance.

RENÉ. Be quiet you old goat! People will hear and I will be shot!

LECLERC. *(Whispering.)* I bring a message from Michelle of the Resistance.

RENÉ. And now I can't hear a word. Can you not strike a happy medium?

LECLERC. I would never hit a cheerful Gypsy! The curse would be…

RENÉ. I mean talk at a normal volume. What is this message?

LECLERC. The message?

RENÉ. The one from Michelle.

LECLERC. You have a message from Michelle? So do I!

RENÉ. Oh for the love of...and what is this message that you have from Michelle?

LECLERC. It is this. Michelle is on her way here with a message for you.

RENÉ. Then why on earth have you come in here? Oh, never mind. It makes as much sense as anything else that happens with the Resistance.

LECLERC. I will tell her the coast is clear.

RENÉ. Tell her what you like, I'm going for a lie-down.

> (**LECLERC** *exits,* **RENÉ** *starts to untie his apron and head off for a rest. As he turns with his back to the café patrons,* **GRUBER** *comes to the bar.*)

(*Muttering to himself.*) What a predicament! What I wouldn't do for money right now.

> (**GRUBER** *gives a polite cough and* **RENÉ** *turns and sees him.*)

Although maybe not that. Can I help you, Lieutenant?

GRUBER. I am sorry that the Colonel is taking such a tough line with you, René. It has left quite a bad taste in my mouth.

RENÉ. Perhaps a cognac, then? (*He pours a glass of cognac from a bottle.*)

GRUBER. Thank you. As you know René, I have come to consider us very good friends. I would hate to see you lying on the ground riddled with bullets.

RENÉ. I can't say I'd enjoy it very much either. But I appreciate your words of kindness.

GRUBER. If there is anything I can do to help, René? I relish these little chats. I often recall them fondly.

RENÉ. (*Quickly.*) We have never fondled, Lieutenant.

GRUBER. Do you have any of those good cigars, René? I recall some finer ones kept under the counter for your better customers.

RENÉ. Sadly, they are all gone, Lieutenant. Although I am expecting a delivery fairly soon. Please excuse me, I am suddenly very tired and need a rest. If the delivery comes along later, and I have the energy, I will slip you one.

GRUBER. *(With keen interest.)* I'll see you later then!

> *(**GRUBER** returns to the **COLONEL**'s table. **RENÉ** exits up the stairs. **EDITH** is approached by **YVETTE** and **MIMI**.)*

YVETTE. René has left looking quite distressed. Is everything alright?

EDITH. He has a lot to think about. The Germans will drop him right in it unless he can pay them fifty thousand francs.

MIMI. Fifty thousand francs! How will he find such a sum?

EDITH. I fear you girls might have to take your evening activities up a notch and put in a little overtime.

YVETTE. Mon Dieu! I am working flat out as it is!

MIMI. I will do what it takes, Madam Edith. I am renowned for refreshing the parts that other women miss.

YVETTE. You? You cannot even reach those parts!

MIMI. What? Why you stuck-up strumpet...

> *(**YVETTE** and **MIMI** begin to tussle. **EDITH** breaks them up.)*

EDITH. Girls! Girls! This is not the time to fight. There is a war on. We must think of a plan to help René.

(**MICHELLE** *enters, dressed in a grubby shirt and dungarees, with oil marks on her face and a wrench in her hand. She ushers the three ladies to the bar.*)

MICHELLE. Listen very carefully. I shall say this only once. The airmen were not picked up by the British planes. I have had to bring them back here.

EDITH. Where are they?

MICHELLE. I snuck them in around the back. Fortunately, we have a new plan. Where is René?

EDITH. He is having a well-deserved lie-down. Tell me the plan, Michelle, and I will see that he gets it.

MIMI. I will also see that he gets it.

YVETTE. And I will give it to him better than anyone!

(**EDITH** *looks suspiciously at the two girls then shrugs it off.*)

MICHELLE. Very well. On Saturday night we have a troupe of dancers coming to Nouvien to put on a free show for the townsfolk. After the show, we will disguise the airmen as dancers, and they will leave with the other performers.

EDITH. Dancers? Performing here? But what about my cabaret! The café patrons will be devastated if I do not sing for them.

MICHELLE. There are more things at stake here than a bruised ego, Madam Edith! We must do our duty to France.

EDITH. You are right, Michelle. And yet, the Resistance also has a duty to my husband, the brave war hero who often risks all to help you.

MICHELLE. And what is it he wants from me?

EDITH. If René does not give the Germans fifty thousand francs by Saturday night he will be shot.

MICHELLE. That would be a shame, but there are other café owners in Nouvien.

EDITH. And what if he were to try to buy his freedom by revealing what he knows about the Resistance?

MICHELLE. Then I would shoot him myself! But this is too big a gamble to take…very well, we will assist him. I will get this money somehow. And how will he explain where he got the money without betraying us?

YVETTE. Why do we not hold a fundraising night on Saturday? We could use your dancers, and Madam Edith's floorshow and pretend that we have raised all the money ourselves?

MIMI. Raise fifty thousand francs with Madam Edith's singing? Are you mad?

EDITH. It is an excellent plan. The Resistance gets what it wants, we get what we want, and everyone wins.

MICHELLE. And we will of course steal the money back from the Germans as soon as possible. I will send word when we have the money. Madam Edith, start practising for this entertainment spectacular.

EDITH. Immediately. *(She opens her mouth and takes a breath to sing.)*

MICHELLE. But wait until I have left first.

> *(**MICHELLE** exits. **MADAM EDITH** looks a tad put out.)*

YVETTE. Madam Edith, Mimi and I must now start to raise what we can in case the Resistance are unsuccessful.

MIMI. *(Motioning towards the **COLONEL** and **GEERING**.)* And with the clientele we have to hand they will take a lot of raising.

EDITH. Of course, girls, do what you must.

> *(YVETTE and MIMI approach the COLONEL at his table.)*

YVETTE. Colonel, how handsome you look tonight. Can I interest you in a little…dessert?

COLONEL. And what is on the trolley?

MIMI. Us. But I must warn you, the prices have gone up due to inflation.

GEERING. Who gets inflated?

YVETTE. You naughty little man.

COLONEL. Very well, ladies. But if we are to pay extra, I insist that I get to use not only the flying helmet and the egg whisk but also the wooden spoons.

MIMI. *(Aside to YVETTE.)* My goodness! Whatever will they be doing with that?

YVETTE. *(Aside to MIMI.)* I'm not sure, Mimi, but I can guarantee it won't be a piece of cake.

> *(The COLONEL and GEERING escort YVETTE and MIMI upstairs, leaving GRUBER to sit alone. EDITH smiles at him.)*

EDITH. And now I must practise. This little number will bring the house down.

> *(EDITH opens her mouth and draws her breath to sing. Blackout.)*

Scene Six
The Funeral Parlour

(A few days later. The undertaker's parlour. There is a single entrance/door. **MONSIEUR ALPHONSE** *is counting out some money. There is a knock on the door and before he can hide the money,* **RENÉ** *and* **EDITH** *enter.* **MONSIEUR ALPHONSE** *greets* **EDITH**, *kissing her hand.)*

ALPHONSE. Ah, Mademoiselle Edith, you are as beautiful as ever.

EDITH. Oh, Monsieur Alphonse, ever the true gentleman.

*(**EDITH** casts a look at **RENÉ**, who studiously ignores it.)*

ALPHONSE. And what can I do for you today, Madam?

RENÉ. Much as it saddens me to admit it, we need your help.

ALPHONSE. Good. Tell me, who is the recently departed? *(He picks up his tape measure lovingly.)*

RENÉ. No-one has died…yet…

ALPHONSE. Ah, it is expected soon is it? I will do a discount if it is money up front.

RENÉ. Oh, charming! And I suppose you get your money back if you don't die?

ALPHONSE. Certainly. After one hundred years I will issue a full refund.

EDITH. Monsieur Alphonse, no-one has died. It is on another matter we come. We are in need of some money and to that end we are putting on a variety night at the Café René, and we would…

ALPHONSE. Ah, Madam, you need say no more. You want me to play the spoons.

RENÉ. The spoons!

ALPHONSE. I was a spoonist in my youth and I carry them with me still, in case of emergency.

> (**ALPHONSE** *whips out a pair of spoons from his top pocket, and starts playing them, appallingly. He stops suddenly.*)

It's a natural gift that I am blessed with. Few are chosen. This is *La Marseillaise* in case you didn't recognise it.

> (**ALPHONSE** *starts again...worse if that's possible.*)

RENÉ. No, no, we don't want you to play the spoons...

ALPHONSE. Ah, the saw then. Let me get it.

> (**ALPHONSE** *starts to go.*)

RENÉ. No, let me finish. Until we have the funds in from the variety night, we have no money, and well, we need some help.

> (**ALPHONSE** *begins to see what he is being asked for and folds his arms.*)

ALPHONSE. Mmm?

EDITH. Monsieur Alphonse. It is known about the town that you are a charming, charitable...

> (**RENÉ** *snorts and* **EDITH** *kicks him quite hard.*)

... And, might I say, handsome man and we knew we could rely on you.

ALPHONSE. Well, I am not a rich man you know.

RENÉ. Not a rich man? You bung together a box, shove someone in it, dig a hole, chuck them down it and charge one thousand francs a time. And in the middle of a world war!

EDITH. René, leave this to me. Monsieur Alphonse, we come to you in hope of a loan.

ALPHONSE. Well, I could loan you ten francs I suppose.

EDITH. Could you make it a little more Monsieur?

ALPHONSE. Well, how much were you looking at?

RENÉ. Fifty thousand francs.

(**ALPHONSE** *clutches his heart. He staggers about dramatically.*)

ALPHONSE. Oh, my dicky ticker!

RENÉ. Is there another undertaker we can call?

(**ALPHONSE** *recovers to some extent.*)

ALPHONSE. What do you need it for?

EDITH. It is to pay off General Von Klinkerhoffen, and the money will be paid back by the Resistance. We will pay it back within the week. *(She starts fluttering her eyelids.)*

ALPHONSE. Well, I suppose I could.

(**ALPHONSE** *pulls a document and pen from his pocket. He writes on the document, leaning on the coffin and hands it to* **RENÉ**.)

RENÉ. *(Reading the contract.)* "Fifty-thousand franc loan to René Artois, for the duration of one week. Seventy five thousand francs to be paid back by next Thursday... cash only..." do you realise how much that is on a daily interest rate?

ALPHONSE. One thousand, three hundred and sixty nine point eight six percent per day.

RENÉ. But this is extortionate! You are a wealthy man…

ALPHONSE. Yes, and I intend to stay that way. Sign please, and then you may go outside and scream.

RENÉ. Edith, you sign.

ALPHONSE. How dare you attempt to impose such a burden on a beautiful lady!

RENÉ. I'm not. I just want my wife to sign it.

ALPHONSE. You are a bounder sir, and a cad.

EDITH. Yes, he is. Sign it!

   (**RENÉ** *signs the contract.*)

RENÉ. It is I who has the dicky ticker now. Now where is the money?

ALPHONSE. I will deliver it to you.

RENÉ. But I need it for Saturday night to give to the General.

ALPHONSE. I do not keep such vast amounts of money here. There are unscrupulous people around you know.

RENÉ. (*Pointedly.*) Yes, aren't there just.

ALPHONSE. I will have it sent round to the café.

RENÉ. Make sure that you do!

EDITH. Well, goodbye Monsieur Alphonse. Until the next time.

   (*They gaze at one another.*)

ALPHONSE. Yes Mademoiselle. If 'twer one second, it would seem like a lifetime to me…

RENÉ. Oh shut up! Come on woman.

   (**RENÉ** *and* **EDITH** *exit. Fade out on a happy looking* **ALPHONSE** *clutching his contract.*)

Scene Seven
René's Café

(The following Saturday night. Lights up on **RENÉ** *who is busy cleaning behind the bar and looking worried. Various French peasants and German soldiers are already in the café.)*

RENÉ. *(Spotting the audience.)* It is now Saturday and in a few minutes time the Colonel and the General will be coming to the café for an evening of quality entertainment and to collect the money. *(Pause.)* I have a problem. Not only do we not yet have any quality entertainment, but I still do not have the money. Monsieur Alphonse has not delivered the promised cash, not that I am too upset since the interest is so high, but if the resistance do not supply the money as agreed I will have to rely on the old swindler. The serving girls have been very supportive and are doing their best to help. It has been a very busy week; we are now completely out of wet celery, and I will not be using the egg whisk to make soufflé any time soon! Even my wife has offered to help but the extra five centimes would not make a difference.

> *(***YVETTE*** *and* ***MIMI*** *enter down the stairs escorting a German soldier. Both girls are wearing flying helmets. The German soldier looks exhausted.)*

MIMI. Goodbye!

YVETTE. Come back again soon!

> *(The German soldier pays some cash to* **YVETTE** *and goes and joins others at a table.* **YVETTE** *hands the money to* **RENÉ** *who adds it*

to money which he takes from the till behind the bar and counts.)

Do we have enough?

RENÉ. Sadly not. *(He continues to count the cash.)*

*(**MIMI** sighs.)*

YVETTE. Why do you sigh, Mimi?

MIMI. It is the life we lead, Yvette. It is terrible. Climbing those stairs time after time to entertain men. It is not right!

YVETTE. Oh, I agree with you. We should have a room on the ground floor.

*(**YVETTE** and **MIMI** move off to attend to the customers. **EDITH** comes down the stairs. She is dressed to impress.)*

RENÉ. Ah, there you are…

EDITH. Do you not like my dress? It is new today from the dress maker. I bought it for a ridiculous figure.

RENÉ. *(Looking her up and down.)* That goes without saying! How are we going to entertain the General this evening?

EDITH. Should I sing a song?

RENÉ. No, we don't want to lose any more customers. Go into the kitchen and do something unforgettable!

EDITH. You haven't said that to me since 1940.

RENÉ. I mean prepare some food!

*(**EDITH** is about to leave when the **COLONEL**, **GEERING** and **GRUBER** enter though the main door.)*

Ah Colonel, Captain, Lieutenant, please take a seat.

COLONEL. Have you got the money for us to give to the General, René?

RENÉ. I am expecting it soon.

COLONEL. I hope for your sake it arrives in time.

RENÉ. Oh, but Colonel, we are old friends, you wouldn't shoot me?

COLONEL. That goes without saying.

RENÉ. I would feel better if you said it, just the same.

GEERING. We won't, but the General will!

RENÉ. That is nice to know…

(**RENÉ** *heads back to the bar looking worried and* **GRUBER** *follows him.*)

GRUBER. I have a little fancy for something from behind the bar.

RENÉ. Mimi or Yvette?

GRUBER. Oh, René. A cognac perhaps. I wish to speak to you, man to man.

RENÉ. Oh yes…

GRUBER. I am very worried about you. You are looking very anxious.

RENÉ. The threat of being shot does that to a man.

GRUBER. I have a wonderful plan. I will take you to my quarters and hide you there until the war is over.

RENÉ. That is a good plan. *(Pause.)* But let us think of a different one…

(*A* **GERMAN SOLDIER** *enters through the main door.*)

SOLDIER. General Von Klinkerhoffen!

RENÉ. Oh 'eck!

(The Germans all jump to attention.)

GENERAL. Heil Hitler!

COLONEL. Heil Hitler!

GRUBER. Heil Hitler!

GEERING. *(Late.)* 'Tler!

RENÉ. Welcome General, what a pleasure to have you here. Yvette, Mimi, champagne for the officers!

> *(**YVETTE** and **MIMI** bring over a tray of glasses and a couple of bottles for the **GERMANS**.)*

May I tell you a little legend, General? It is said that these champagne glasses were modelled on the bosom of Marie Antoinette.

GEERING. They should have modelled them on Yvette's bosom. We would have got a bigger drink.

RENÉ. So, General, how is the war going? Do you have the half-time score?

GENERAL. You know why I am here. I have been promised entertainment. *(Turning to the **COLONEL** and **GEERING**.)* And then you will give me my money.

RENÉ. Oh yes…the entertainment, one moment General…

> *(**MICHELLE** and **CRABTREE** enter. **CRABTREE** carries a bag of dancing girl costumes.)*

Do you have to come in here? The place is crawling with Germans!

MICHELLE. Listen very carefully, he will say this only once…

RENÉ. That is a pity as I can never understand him!

CRABTREE. I have good nose and bad nose.

RENÉ. Better have the good *nose* first!

CRABTREE. You are in lick. The Resistance have committed a cream!

YVETTE. A cream?

CRABTREE. Yes a cream. You know like minslaughter, roop and arsin?

RENÉ. Oh yes, those are very nasty creams.

CRABTREE. They have ribbed a bonk!

MICHELLE. Fifty thousand francs!

RENÉ. Well, hand it over then...

MICHELLE. There is a problem.

CRABTREE. Now for the bad nose...

MICHELLE. We could not bring it here ourselves...

RENÉ. Yes, that would be too simple.

MICHELLE. ...So we gave it to the dancers to bring with them...

CRABTREE. ...But now the con-con girls have din a rooner. *(He indicates the bag of costumes.)*

MICHELLE. They have disappeared from their hotel. Only their costumes remain. I fear they are not coming. So good luck! We will now disappear like...

RENÉ. Oh, no you won't. You helped get me in to this mess and you can help get me out of this. How are your legs?

MICHELLE. My legs?

RENÉ. Yes. The General is expecting Can-Can dancers and you and this English idiot can join us in providing the replacements...

*(The **GENERAL** calls from his table.)*

GENERAL. Peasant! Entertain us!

RENÉ. Soon, Herr General, soon! *(To* **EDITH.***)* Edith, I never thought I would say this but I need you to sing for us while we get ready...

EDITH. I will distract them! Tonight, I will sing as I have never done before!

RENÉ. In tune?

> *(***RENÉ** *ushers* **CRABTREE, MICHELLE, YVETTE, MIMI** *and* **LECLERC** *off into the back room, to get changed for their Can-Can leaving* **EDITH** *to entertain the café.)*

EDITH. Good evening, ladies and gentlemen. We are delighted to have been ordered here to perform for you this evening. I will start with a little musical number...

> *(Sound effects: Music for* **EDITH.*** **EDITH** *begins to sing and everyone reacts by stuffing cheese/bread and anything else to hand into their ears. The* **COLONEL** *and* **GEERING** *have come prepared and have cheese pieces in their pockets. The* **GENERAL** *is not prepared and sits dumbfounded though the song.* **EDITH** *finishes her song with a flourish. There is a less than enthusiastic reaction from the audience.)*

GENERAL. Unforgettable!

GEERING. René's wife has many talents.

GRUBER. Singing is not one of them.

> *(The* **COLONEL** *removes the cheese from his ear and looks at it.)*

---

* A licence to produce *'Allo 'Allo 2* does not include a performance license for any third-party or copyrighted music. Licensees should create an original composition or use music in the public domain. For further information, please see the Music Use Note on page iii.

COLONEL. What sort of cheese is this?

GEERING. Gruyère, I think.

COLONEL. I mustn't use it again. There are too many holes!

> (**HERR FLICK** and **HELGA** enter disguised as onion sellers with moustaches and berets. **HERR FLICK** also carries a bag [containing his hat]. **EDITH** greets them and shows them to a table.)

EDITH. Oh, I am afraid you have just missed my singing.

FLICK. That is good news for we are music lovers. Come He... (He realises he may give the game away.) Come Henri...let us sit over here.

> (**EDITH** moves away from the table as **HERR FLICK** and **HELGA** sit.)

FLICK. I know this must be exciting for you.

HELGA. (Suggestively.) It is not the first time I have been *undercover* with you Herr Flick.

FLICK. Do not be a smart Alec Helga and get ideas above your station.

HELGA. In these clothes we are equal!

FLICK. On the contrary! My onions are bigger than your onions, and I have two rows. Now we sit and wait and see if we can spot the British airmen.

> (**EDITH** moves back to the **GENERAL**'s table.)

GENERAL. Your voice reminds me of my boyhood in Bavaria.

EDITH. Oh, you mean like the golden maidens who sing in the cornfields?

GENERAL. No, the threshing machine.

EDITH. I'm sure you fancy a little sophisticated company to while away a leisurely hour? A man like you should always have at his side a beautiful woman!

GENERAL. I agree…but sometimes the roulette wheel of life throws up the odd zero.

EDITH. Of course, I do not sit with ordinary soldiers although they crave my company.

GENERAL. Hmmm. When it is wartime men, a long way from home, get very desperate.

EDITH. Are you desperate General?

GENERAL. Not yet! Give us more entertainment!

> (**EDITH** *clears her voice to start singing once more.*)

But no more singing!

> (**RENÉ** *enters from the back room, now suitable dressed for dancing.*)

RENÉ. Coming Gen… (*He changes to a falsetto voice.*) Coming General!

> (**MICHELLE**, **CRABTREE**, **CARSTAIRS**, **FAIRFAX**, **MIMI** *and* **YVETTE** *enter from the back room in Can-Can costumes and form a dance line centre stage. The men wear wigs as part of the disguise.*)

EDITH. And now for your delight; the Can-Can girls of Nancy!

> (*Sound effects: Can-Can music*. The 'girls' dance and the audience claps along with the*

---

* A license to produce *'Allo 'Allo 2* does not include a performance license for any third-party or copyrighted music. Licensees should create an original composition or use music in the public domain. For further information, please see the Music and Third-Party Materials Use Note on page iii.

officers clearly enjoying the display of legs. **GRUBER** *is watching the show with very little interest until he recognises* **RENÉ**. *He waves at* **RENÉ** *throughout the rest of the dance. The dance ends and there is much applause. The dancers disperse to mingle with the guests.)*

GERMANS. Bravo, encore *(Etc!)*

FAIRFAX. Carstairs, you're standing like a tart again.

(**CARSTAIRS** *drops his arm to his side.*)

EDITH. *(To* **RENÉ**, *looking the* **BRITISH AIRMEN** *up and down.)* No one will suspect them. They look just like the staff.

RENÉ. Edith, the Germans *take* the staff upstairs from time to time. If they took these two upstairs, do you not think that their suspicions will be aroused?

YVETTE. We are much more attractive. They will take us.

RENÉ. Better to be on the safe side…

(**RENÉ** *mimes to the* **BRITISH AIRMEN** *that they must not go upstairs with the* **GERMANS**.)

CARSTAIRS. *(Turning to* **FAIRFAX**.*)* What was all that about?

FAIRFAX. I think he means that if the Germans want us to go upstairs with them, we're not to go.

(**RENÉ** *turns to the* **BRITISH AIRMEN** *and mimes that they must be silent.)*

CARSTAIRS. What does that mean?

FAIRFAX. Well, if we do go upstairs with the Krauts, we're not to tell anyone.

CARSTAIRS. Well, it's hardly the sort of thing you boast about, is it.

*(The 'dancers' disperse and start fraternising with the clientele. **RENÉ** comes over to the bar and is accosted by **GRUBER**.)*

GRUBER. I wish to speak to you confidentially. Can you bend over a little?

RENÉ. I would prefer not to Lieutenant.

GRUBER. Good evening René. I'd recognise those legs anywhere. But do not worry, your secret is safe with me.

RENÉ. No, you do not understand...

GRUBER. Oh I think I do my dear René. I had an uncle with similar leanings. Every Shrove Tuesday he would dress up as a pancake girl!

> *(**HERR FLICK** has been watching the dancers with interest.)*

FLICK. Do you notice anything strange Helga?

HELGA. Strange, Herr Flick?

FLICK. I have my suspicions. It is time for us to intervene. *(He stands up and limps forward.)* Stand where you are! No-one is to move!

GENERAL. What is the meaning of this interruption! Sit down, peasant or you will be shot.

FLICK. It is I, Herr Flick of the Gestapo!

> *(The **GENERAL** look at him disbelieving. **FLICK** removes his beret and false moustache and pull his hat from his bag and puts it on his head. The transformation is immediate.)*

GENERAL. How dare you intrude upon this little party!

FLICK. There is no reason to cease your jollification just because a senior Gestapo officer in a particularly foul mood is here. I have reason to believe that within this café there are British airmen masquerading as women. I wish to interrogate these dancers…

GENERAL. What nonsense!

FLICK. Line up! Quickly!

> *(The dancers line up, the ladies at the right end of the line, then **CRABTREE**, **RENÉ**, and the two **BRITISH AIRMEN**. **FLICK** walks down the line and peers at each in turn. The ladies flaunt themselves; it is quite clear to **HERR FLICK** and everyone else that they are women. **HERR FLICK** looks a little sheepish.)*

GENERAL. Have you finished?

> *(**HERR FLICK** has reached **CRABTREE**, who looks back innocently.)*

FLICK. Good evening Frauline.

CRABTREE. Good moaning.

FLICK. That is an unusual accent? What part of France do you come from?

CRABTREE. I am half Itoolian.

FLICK. Itoolian?

HELGA. I think he means Italian.

CRABTREE. Yes. I was brought up in Nipples.

FLICK. *(To the **GERMAN OFFICERS**.)* Do you not notice anything strange about this dancer?

COLONEL. She has very large feet?

FLICK. And has a moustache?

GEERING. That is not unusual for a French girl…

FLICK. *(Pulling off **CRABTREE**'s wig.)* Aha! As I thought! One of the airmen…

RENÉ. *(Pulling off his wig.)* Herr Flick, General, forgive me, I must explain. A couple of the dancing girls were indisposed and so we had to replace them. This kind gentleman, who is a policeman in this town, agreed to wear the dress for the dance. *(To* **CRABTREE**.*)* Thank you officer...

CRABTREE. A Policemon's lit is not a hippy one.

FLICK. But?

GENERAL. Herr Flick, you are exceeding your authority. This is a private party. The Gestapo has no jurisdiction over senior officers of the German Army.

GEERING. Or junior officers.

RENÉ. What about café owners?

GEERING. They can do what they like with them!

GENERAL. Enough of this. Herr Flick. I order you to leave.

FLICK. You will regret this. *(With menace.)* My godfather is Heinrick Himmler.

GENERAL. And my wife's sister is the mistress of Hermann Goering. The one who wears the chamois leather underclothes.

FLICK. *(Deflating somewhat.)* I see. That changes things...

GENERAL. I'm warning you; Do not attempt to cross me again – you'll be kept under very close observation. Berlin will also be informed of your perverse antics and your recalcitrant demeanour, which has exacerbated the quid pro quo, vis-à-vis inter-departmental relationships.

FLICK. Come, Helga. To our dictionaries!

*(***HERR FLICK** *and* **HELGA** *exit.)*

RENÉ. More champagne for the General?

(**YVETTE** *takes a bottle to the table. The atmosphere picks up again and the* **GERMAN OFFICERS** *fraternise with the dancers.* **YVETTE** *and* **MIMI** *are flirting with* **GEERING** *and the* **COLONEL**. *The* **BRITISH AIRMEN** *manage to get themselves on either side of the* **GENERAL** *who is clearly enjoying their company.* **CRABTREE** *and* **MICHELLE** *have managed to blend into the background.* **RENÉ** *and* **EDITH** *look worried.*)

Where is that undertaker with the money he promised us? If he does not come quick, there is not going to be a wall in Nouvion big enough to shoot us against!

EDITH. René, if they'd shoot us, at least I would die at your side.

RENÉ. If you died in front of me, at least I'd have a better chance.

(**RENÉ** *crosses back to the table.*)

GENERAL. So Colonel do you have for me my money?

COLONEL. Errr... (*Nervously.*) the café owner has been looking after it for us...

GENERAL. Most unorthodox... (*To* **RENÉ**.) Never mind, it can wait...

RENÉ. Wait?

GENERAL. I have had a thoroughly agreeable evening even with the interruption. I will return for the money in the morning.

RENÉ. Very well...

GENERAL. And for now, I will take these charming girls back to the chateau to continue the party? What do you say girls?

BRITISH AIRMEN. What?!

RENÉ. Oh, but they are young innocent things General, and their parents are expecting them home before ten o'clock.

GENERAL. Nonsense! Perhaps a bottle of your finest brandy to take with us.

RENÉ. Of course... *(He crosses to the bar.)* What are we going to do?

> *(**LECLERC** enters. He carries a tray overloaded with cheeses including several camembert.)*

LECLERC. Camembert, get your camembert here.

RENÉ. What are you doing you nitwit?

LECLERC. It is I, Leclerc!

RENÉ. We know it is you, Leclerc, man of a thousand faces, everyone the same. What are you doing here? This is not a good time!

LECLERC. I am surreptitiously selling camembert.

RENÉ. To what end may I ask? I have a café full of cheese from my normal supplier.

LECLERC. One of them is for you, from the undertaker. It has *something* in it *(He winks unsubtly.)*

RENÉ. Good, give me the cheese.

LECLERC. No, no. You must *buy* it from me. We need to keep the subterfuge realistic.

RENÉ. Oh, dear me. Oh, all right. *(Loudly.)* Ah Monsieur camembert seller. Could I purchase from you a lovely cheese?

LECLERC. Certainly, Monsieur customer. Which one would you like?

RENÉ. *(Quietly.)* I don't know you incompetent fool! Only you know which one I must have.

LECLERC. *(Quietly.)* Oh yes. *(Loudly.)* Shall I guide you to the best deal today, Monsieur?

RENÉ. *(Quietly.)* They are all the same you idiot.

LECLERC. Oh yes. They are all…um…one franc each.

RENÉ. I will have one please, cheese seller. Whichever one you think best.

(LECLERC hesitates and looks down.)

LECLERC. I cannot remember which one it is.

(GRUBER wanders over.)

GRUBER. I may buy one of them at that price…they look tasty.

COLONEL. *(Calling from the table.)* And me…

GEERING. *(Calling from the table.)* Yes, I too will have one.

GENERAL. *(Calling from the table.)* I will have four at that price.

LECLERC. *(To the GERMANS.)* Certainly. *(To RENÉ.)* Sorry René, I have sold out.

RENÉ. *(Quietly.)* You are not supposed to be selling them.

LECLERC. But René, I am a cheese seller!

RENÉ. You are not. You are a twit. You are supposed to be giving me the cheese which the undertaker gave you.

LECLERC. Oh yes. I got carried away.

RENÉ. Sadly not by the undertaker. Right I shall have to take action. *(To everyone.)* Ladies and gentlemen at such a good price I, René, will buy all of them and we will have a cheese party.

COLONEL. Oooh, hand them out then René.

RENÉ. Ah, no, I have to check them first, quality control.

COLONEL. Quality control has not been a problem in the past?

RENÉ. But times they are a-changing, Colonel, and some people use the situation to take advantage of struggling businessmen. I do not include you amongst those men, of course, as I do not want to be shot. I have to vet the wines we buy, I have to vet the food we buy…

GEERING. And your entertainment?

RENÉ. I have Yvette for that too.

GENERAL. Less lollygagging! Hand out those cheeses and we will continue this fine evening. I do not like to be kept waiting.

RENÉ. Just checking the cheeses, General.

GENERAL. *(Drawing his pistol and threatening* **RENÉ**.*)* Now!

> *(***RENÉ*** snaps his fingers; everyone freezes. Light spot on* **RENÉ**.*)*

RENÉ. Now, this is a pretty predicament. I now have a dozen camembert cheeses, one of which contains fifty thousand francs which I must give to the General. I don't know which one contains the money, and although my clients generally like their cheese a little rich, that particular one might be overegging the pudding. That is probably enough cookery metaphors so instead I will follow my instincts and assume the lightest cheese will be hollow and contain the money.

> *(***RENÉ*** snaps his fingers again; everyone unfreezes. Lights up on all.)*

Please, Herr General, holster your weapon. The cheese is ready.

GENERAL. Then this evening we party *(Drops voice to more stern tone.)* and tomorrow we will complete our business.

RENÉ. *(To audience.)* Between the German's risky business, the resistance's funny business and Edith's attempts at show business I am quite spent. Why don't you pop off for a quick interval?

> *(Blackout. Curtain. Sound effects: " 'Allo 'Allo" theme music.* End of Act One.)*

---

* A licence to produce *'Allo 'Allo 2* does not include a performance licence for "'Allo 'Allo theme music". The publisher and author suggest that the licensee contact PRS to ascertain the music publisher and contact such music publisher to license or acquire permission for performance of the song. If a licence or permission is unattainable for "'Allo 'Allo theme music", the licensee may not use the song in *'Allo 'Allo 2* but should create an original composition in a similar style or use a similar song in the public domain. For further information, please see the Music and Third-Party Materials Use Note on page iii.

ACT TWO

Scene One
René's Café

(The following Monday morning. Sound effects: "'Allo 'Allo" theme music. Lights up on the Café.* **RENÉ** *is alone behind the bar, pouring himself a drink.)*

RENÉ. Hello again. It is now Monday morning. When we last met, I had a gaggle of Germans, a disorder of dancers and a confusion of camembert cheeses in the café! To save my skin I had to hand over the cheese with the fifty thousand francs to the General to distract him, so he did not elope with the British airmen. Monsieur Alphonse is expecting me to pay him back with interest by Thursday. The Resistance were supposed to bring me the money but it has disappeared so I now cannot repay the undertaker. The British airman may have escaped a fate worse than death; an evening with General Von Klinkerhoffen but that is the only escaping they have managed so far. The Gestapo

---

* A licence to produce *'Allo 'Allo 2* does not include a performance licence for "'Allo 'Allo theme music". The publisher and author suggest that the licensee contact PRS to ascertain the music publisher and contact such music publisher to license or acquire permission for performance of the song. If a licence or permission is unattainable for "'Allo 'Allo theme music", the licensee may not use the song in *'Allo 'Allo 2* but should create an original composition in a similar style or use a similar song in the public domain. For further information, please see the Music and Third-Party Materials Use Note on page iii..

correctly suspect that they are here. In short, it is looking up to be a miserable week!

> (**CRABTREE**, **MICHELLE** *and the* **BRITISH AIRMEN** *enter through the front door.*
>
> *The* **BRITISH AIRMEN** *are once more in French peasant costume.*)

And I suspect it is about to get worse...

CRABTREE. *(In a British accent to the* **BRITISH AIRMEN**.*)* Wait here chaps, we need to speak to the Frenchie...

BRITISH AIRMEN. Jolly good! *(Etc.)*

> *(The* **BRITISH AIRMEN** *take a seat at a table.)*

CRABTREE. *(Crossing to* **RENÉ**.*)* Good Moaning!

RENÉ. *(Resignedly.)* Good Moaning!

MICHELLE. Listen very carefully, I will say this only once.

RENÉ. What?

MICHELLE. I will say this only once.

RENÉ. No, what will you say?

MICHELLE. There is still no sign of the dancers.

RENÉ. They probably ran off with the money and who can blame them?

MICHELLE. So, the Resistance cannot give you the fifty thousand francs.

RENÉ. But this mean I cannot repay Monsieur Alphonse. And what about those airmen? You heard Herr Flick, the other night, he suspects that they are here...

MICHELLE. The Gestapo are wicked men who will stop at nothing. They may even arrest your wife and torture her in front of you to make you speak.

RENÉ. I will grit my teeth bravely and tell them nothing.

CRABTREE. Do not wirry Ronnie. We have a plin.

RENÉ. Oh and what is the latest hare-brained *plin* to get them back to Britain? Are they sending a midget submarine up the sewers?

MICHELLE. *(Alarmed.)* That was supposed to be a secret! No, we are working on a new plan. We shall now disappear like phantoms into the night...

CRABTREE. We will goo out the bock wee.

   *(**CRABTREE** beckons to the **BRITISH AIRMEN**.)*

FAIRFAX. Oh! Can't we stay for a cup of tea?

RENÉ. Get out!

CARSTAIRS. Oh!

   *(**MICHELLE**, **CRABTREE** and the **BRITISH AIRMEN** exit through the side door.)*

RENÉ. Wonderful, wonderful! Mimi!

   *(**MIMI** enters down the stairs.)*

MIMI. What is it René?

RENÉ. It is not good news. The Resistance have lost the money and now I cannot repay Monsieur Alphonse...

MIMI. Do you want me to kill him for you?

RENÉ. No Mimi! For a start, there will be no undertaker around to bury him.

MIMI. Oh, René, hold me!

   *(**RENÉ** and **MIMI** embrace.)*

RENÉ. You have no idea what the feel of your firm young body does to me!

MIMI. Yes, I have!

RENÉ. Oh, my little cauliflower!

MIMI. My aubergine!

RENÉ. My broccoli floret!

MIMI. Oh, my butternut squash!

RENÉ. Oh, Mimi, when we are too old to make love, we will make wonderful soup.

MIMI. René, night after night I dream that you come to my room. You hold me in your arms, you kiss me. You make wild, abandoned love to me. When are we going to be together?

RENÉ. With dreams like that, you hardly need me!

MIMI. Do you not ache for me, just a little bit?

RENÉ. From time to time, I do get a little bit stiff but I put it down to age.

> (**MONSIEUR ALPHONSE** *enters through the main door and catches* **RENÉ** *canoodling with* **MIMI**.)

ALPHONSE. What is this?

> (**RENÉ** *and* **MIMI** *react.* **MIMI** *quickly brushes herself off and exits, embarrassed, through the side door.*)

What of Madame Edith? From now on, monsieur, the gloves are off and I will press my suit. I intend telling her everything I've seen.

RENÉ. Oh, but, Monsieur Alphonse, a Frenchman does not tell on another Frenchman.

ALPHONSE. It is true. But I have Belgian blood on my mother's side.

RENÉ. Monsieur Alphonse, this is probably not a good time to mention it but I cannot repay the loan.

ALPHONSE. We had an agreement!

RENÉ. I know but it is difficult.

ALPHONSE. In that case, Monsieur, since you are a man without honour... *(He takes off a glove and slaps it around* **RENÉ**'s *face.)*

RENÉ. What was that for?

ALPHONSE. I challenge you to a duel.

RENÉ. A duel?

ALPHONSE. I warn you that I am a crack shot and have put one of my balls through a playing card at twenty-five paces.

RENÉ. I'm surprised you don't walk with a limp.

ALPHONSE. And once you are dead then perhaps Madame Edith will make me the happiest man alive?

RENÉ. I thought you wanted to marry her?

ALPHONSE. What will be the time and the place?

RENÉ. Can I suggest South America, the Christmas after next?

ALPHONSE. I will return tomorrow night when I shall rid France of a bounder and a cad.

*(***MONSIEUR ALPHONSE*** crosses to leave by the main door. As he does so,* **YVETTE**, *comes in the main door carrying some shopping.)*

YVETTE. Oh Monsieur, are you looking for a naughty girl to give you a good time?

ALPHONSE. Please! Mademoiselle! I am a well-respected member of this community, a pillar of society, a cornerstone of the establishment! How much?

RENÉ. I doubt your dicky ticker could handle it.

ALPHONSE. *(To **RENÉ**.)* Until tomorrow! I shall start preparing a coffin.

> (**ALPHONSE** *exits through the main door.* **YVETTE** *crosses to* **RENÉ**.)

YVETTE. What are you doing tomorrow?

RENÉ. After he has finished with me, very little! He is going to shoot me because I cannot pay my debts.

YVETTE. Oh René!

> *(They embrace.)*

One touch of you and I go limp all over…

RENÉ. I hope it is not contagious!

> (**EDITH** *enters down the stairs and sees* **RENÉ** *and* **YVETTE** *mid clinch.*)

EDITH. René! What are you doing with your arms around that serving girl?

RENÉ. You stupid woman? Can you not see she's suffering from claustrophobia? She accidentally locked herself in the larder.

EDITH. But there is no key!

RENÉ. Exactly, that's why she couldn't get out.

EDITH. Oh, the poor child. It happened to me once. I screamed and screamed, but nobody came.

RENÉ. We thought you were singing.

YVETTE. Oh Madame Edith, what are we to do? The undertaker is going to shoot René because he cannot pay the debt.

EDITH. Would you like me to sing a song to soothe your nerves?

RENÉ. Well, they do say that one pain can cancel out another.

EDITH. I know, we will have to rob the town bank.

RENÉ. We cannot rob the town bank. The Resistance have already done that! If the bank gets robbed any more, they'll have to put a revolving door on the vault. We need a better plan.

EDITH. I am sure as a brave hero of France you will come up with one… Come Yvette, let us get that food into the kitchen.

> (**EDITH** *hustles off* **YVETTE** *through the side door, leaving* **RENÉ** *alone to consider his options.*)

RENÉ. *(Pause.)* I have come up with a plan. *(Pause.)* I shall investigate the escape route to Switzerland and run away with Yvette! Where is the notepaper? *(He takes out a pen and paper from behind the bar and writes out a note.)* "Dearest love, we must leave Nouvien tonight. Meet me at the train station and we will elope to Switzerland on the six o'clock express. I will book us a sleeper compartment…" *(He moves away from the bar and then has a second thought.)* Oh, and I had better write a tender note to Edith to say goodbye: "Goodbye". *(Pause.)* "I think it is for the best. Do not grieve for me. Monsieur Alphonse will make a fine husband." Right, the one for Yvette in the brown envelope and the one for Edith in the white. *(He puts the notes in the respective envelopes.)* Now to find a messenger to deliver them. Someone I can trust implicitly.

> (**LECLERC** *enters through the main doors.*)

But then again…needs must! *(To* **LECLERC**.*)* Come over here!

LECLERC. It is…

RENÉ. *(Interrupting.)* Yes…yes…we know. Now pay attention, this is very important.

LECLERC. I shall listen very carefully…

RENÉ. *(Interrupting again.)* Don't *you* start! I have here two messages for you to deliver. You must give this note in the *brown* envelope to Yvette.

LECLERC. The one in the buff for your bit of stuff.

RENÉ. Watch it! And do not forget to give the other one to my wife. I must go and pack…

*(**RENÉ** exits upstairs.)*

LECLERC. Right…to deliver the notes…errr…the one in the buff for the old bit of rough. The one in the white for the bit of alright. Simple!

(Blackout.)

Scene Two
The Colonel's HQ

*(The same day. The **COLONEL** is sitting at the desk in his office. **GEERING** stomps in and sits in a chair looking cross.)*

COLONEL. A bad day at the office Captain?

GEERING. Yes Herr Colonel. We have a new intake of privates at the barracks. They are very badly trained and when they are given the order to stand to attention they stand at ease. When they are told to stand at ease, they fall out.

*(**GRUBER** enters and notices the despondent air.)*

GRUBER. Trouble?

COLONEL. It is the Captain. He is having trouble with his privates.

GRUBER. Oh?

GEERING. Yes, they keep falling out.

GRUBER. Have you tried a change of trousers?

COLONEL. This war is not turning out as I expected. I hear too that Hitler is acting strangely.

GEERING. Do you think he has a screw loose?

COLONEL. If you ask me, a whole meccano set has fallen apart in there! I always thought we'd have an easy life, line our pockets well and have a comfortable future after the war. Instead, we have no painting and the General has fifty thousand francs which he won't be sharing with us.

GEERING. It does not seem fair!

COLONEL. It is not. Gruber, you have been to Staff College, how do you sneak into in a General's dressing room?

GRUBER. Hmmm... I think I must have been away that day!

COLONEL. That is unfortunate because I am ordering you to visit Von Klinkerhoffen tonight, distract him and steal back the camembert cheese and the money!

GRUBER. But what if I am caught?

COLONEL. Then you will probably be shot.

GRUBER. Well, if I am, I should like to be buried with Hubert junior.

GEERING. Which regiment is he in?

GRUBER. He's my little tank! Even if I do get away with it, won't the General be very cross when he finds the money has been taken?

COLONEL. We can just blame it on the resistance and shoot a few peasants.

GRUBER. Very well. I shall wear my special cologne.

GEERING. Special cologne?

GRUBER. Lily of the valley with a splash of diesel oil.

COLONEL. Good luck Lieutenant.

GEERING. You'll need it...

(Blackout.)

Scene Three
The Railway Station

(The railway station later that evening. There is a platform sign. Smoke from the trains and suitable lighting set the scene. Sound effects: Steam train sounds and whistle. RENÉ enters carrying a suitcase and looking furtive.)

RENÉ. Pssssttttt!

(YVETTE comes on from the other side.)

YVETTE. René!

RENÉ. Yvette!

YVETTE. Oh René! Kiss me as you have never kissed me before.

RENÉ. That will not be easy.

(RENÉ and YVETTE embrace briefly and then break apart.)

YVETTE. Why are you leaving me?

RENÉ. I am not leaving you! You are coming with me!

YVETTE. But your note? I do not want to marry Monsieur Alphonse.

RENÉ. Why am I thinking that that bunging fool Leclerc has bungled?

(EDITH enters, carrying a suitcase.)

EDITH. René! Why is Yvette here at the train station?

RENÉ. She was distraught to hear that we were leaving and wanted to say goodbye.

EDITH. *(To YVETTE.)* Well, say goodbye quickly as we have a train to catch.

RENÉ. Well, yes, actually, I have had second thoughts about this Edith.

EDITH. What? You do not love me?

RENÉ. Of course, my love, but I do not think it is right to leave now. We have to get the money back from the General so we can repay the undertaker.

EDITH. But what can we do?

RENÉ. I was going to ask this brave girl, to visit the General at his Headquarters, seduce him and steal the money.

EDITH. But how can this innocent girl seduce a general?

YVETTE. I will do my best Madame Edith.

> (**CRABTREE** and **MICHELLE** enter looking furtive.)

CRABTREE. Good Moaning!

RENÉ. It is evening. Your sense of time is even worse than your ability to speak our language.

CRABTREE. My French cod be butter.

MICHÈLLE. Is the coast clear?

RENÉ. We are fifty miles from the coast! How would I know? What are you two doing here?

CRABTREE. We have new escape plin for the British earmen. Watch as I summon them with my pilicemin's wossle...

> (**CRABTREE** blows his whistle and the two **BRITISH AIRMEN** enter dressed as a pantomime horse.)

RENÉ. Oh, my god!

EDITH. But where are the airmen?

CRABTREE. One earman is in the hod.

(**FAIRFAX** *sticks his head out of the horse's head or at least sticks a hand out and waves.*)

FAIRFAX. Hello!

CRABTREE. The other is in the bittim.

(**CARSTAIRS** *sticks his head out of the horse's rear or at least sticks a hand out and waves.*)

CARSTAIRS. Hello! I say it's awfully stuffy in here.

MICHELLE. *(Talking into the horse's bottom.)* Never mind chaps. It won't be long now.

CARSTAIRS. Yes, but I wish we hadn't had onion soup for tea!

(*Sound effects: A loud fart.*)

FAIRFAX. Sorry.

CRABTREE. We do not want them to be spitted by the Nitzis. Is it not a cinning disgeeze?

RENÉ. Oh very cinning.

MICHELLE. Listen very carefully, I will say this only once.

EDITH. Have you ever said anything twice?

MICHELLE. I have, but only once. *(Pause.)* The airmen will travel to Spain on that railway truck *(She gestures to the wings.)* with a cargo of real horses.

YVETTE. But what about the smell?

MICHELLE. I don't think the other horses will mind.

CRABTREE. Is it not a brilliant plin?

RENÉ. I think I see a complicoction. *(Pointing to the wings.)* That truck is carrying young stallions. *(Pointing at the* **BRITISH AIRMEN** *in their costume.)* And that is a lady horse…

CRABTREE. Oh bigger! Back to the drewing board!

(**CRABTREE** *leads the horse off.*)

MICHELLE. René, we in the resistance are feeling bad about the money.

RENÉ. We were just discussing it. Yvette will steal it back.

MICHELLE. There is a flaw in your plan.

RENÉ. Look who's talking!

MICHELLE. The General would miss the money. We need to leave a substitute.

EDITH. But where can we get *another* fifty thousand francs?

MICHELLE. Simple, we have asked Monsieur Leclerc to forge the money and deliver it here in an identical cheese.

YVETTE. What if he is spotted?

MICHELLE. He will come disguised as a mountaineer...

RENÉ. But the nearest mountains are hundreds of miles away!

MICHELLE. He is lost. Naturally he will come to us, to ask for directions.

RENÉ. Naturally...

(**LECLERC** *enters carrying a second large false camembert cheese [filled with forged bank notes]. He is dressed up as a mountaineer complete with hat and ropes. He makes an elaborate display trying not to look suspicious.*)

LECLERC. It is I, Leclerc.

RENÉ. I see you have come as the village idiot. I congratulate you on your most convincing disguise yet.

Let me have a look at this! *(He opens the cheese and pulls out some of the forged notes.)* What is this? The pictures are all wrong and since when is there a ninety-nine franc note?

LECLERC. It was done in a hurry. What do you expect?

RENÉ. You are a useless idiot!

LECLERC. I am a master forger and I have the certificates to prove it!

EDITH. Oh, it will have it do. Yvette, take the cheese and good luck!

*(**YVETTE** takes the cheese and exits.)*

MICHELLE. I have not told you the rest of the plan. Inside the cheese, beneath the money, is a bomb.

RENÉ. A bomb?

MICHELLE. Yes. We will blow up the General and his headquarters.

RENÉ. What!

MICHELLE. There is a special detonation device. Monsieur Leclerc built it and is waiting for the signal!

LECLERC. Now? *(He fumbles in his pockets for the detonator.)*

MICHELLE. No!

RENÉ. *He* made it? Well, of course it will work perfectly!

EDITH. What if it explodes while Yvette is carrying it?

MICHELLE. Then she will be buried as a heroine of the resistance.

RENÉ. First you will have to scrape her off the walls. No Michelle, this is not a good plan.

MICHELLE. What is wrong with it?

RENÉ. Imagine what the Germans will do if you blow up their general! I must go and stop Yvette and bring that cheese back before she gets hurt.

> (**RENÉ** *exits in the same direction that* **YVETTE** *went. Blackout.*)

Scene Four
Herr Flick's Dungeon

(The same evening. **HERR FLICK** *is seated behind his desk eating his lunch. He has a boiled egg which he hammers several times with a spoon. It cracks.)*

FLICK. You see…they always crack in zee end.

(There is a knock at the door.)

Enter!

*(***HELGA*** enters.)*

You are late, Helga.

HELGA. I was delayed by a peasant.

FLICK. Did you shoot him?

HELGA. No, no. I spoke to him sharply and told him to be more careful in future.

FLICK. I sometimes wonder if you are suited for the Gestapo.

HELGA. But, Herr Flick, I didn't know you had girls in the Gestapo?

FLICK. Who do you think types the threatening letters? Here, have this.

*(***HERR FLICK*** hands ***HELGA*** an envelope.)*

HELGA. What is this Herr Flick?

FLICK. Open it. It is your guest membership card for the Gestapo Club, are you pleased?

HELGA. Of course, Herr Flick. To be in the club with the Gestapo will be a great honour.

FLICK. At the Gestapo club we have sausages, frankfurters, beer and sauerkraut. There are always a lot of big noises there.

HELGA. I can imagine there would be.

FLICK. You will also have to learn the Gestapo song: *(He sings it to the tune of the "Hokey Cokey" and does a dance to the words.)*

> 'YOU PUT YOUR RIGHT BOOT IN, YOU TAKE YOUR RIGHT BOOT OUT, YOU DO A LOT OF SHOUTING AND YOU SHAKE YOUR FISTS ABOUT. YOU LIGHT A LITTLE SMOKIE AND YOU BURN DOWN ZE TOWN, ZAT'S VOT IT'S ALL ABOUT. AH, HIMMLER, HIMMLER, HIMMLER ...'

HELGA. *(Interrupting.)* I will have to practice Herr Flick.

FLICK. Indeed. *(Pause.)* I have also decided to marry you.

HELGA. Oh, but Herr Flick, I thought we were going to wait until after the war.

FLICK. These are dangerous times, Helga. We must grab every moment of happiness while we can.

HELGA. Herr Flick, you have always managed to grab it so far *without* getting married.

FLICK. But first I need to know that I can trust you.

HELGA. Trust me Herr Flick?

FLICK. I am well aware that you have loyalties to the Colonel and the others.

HELGA. Of course, not Herr Flick.

FLICK. *(Ignoring her.)* And sometimes I notice you are very close to Lieutenant Gruber.

HELGA. Believe me Herr Flick, Lieutenant Gruber is not very keen on women of the opposite sex! But if you do not trust me Herr Flick, what sort of life will we have when we are married?

FLICK. I will keep you on a short lead.

HELGA. You make me feel like a…wild animal.

FLICK. The feeling is mutual.

HELGA. Take me Herr Flick, I am in the flood of my youth!

FLICK. This I can see. In fact, some of it is spilling over. You may kiss me.

> *(They kiss.* **HELGA** *passionately,* **HERR FLICK** *without any sign of emotion or indeed any response. They break apart.)*

(He considers.) Six out of ten. I have a job for you to prove your loyalty.

HELGA. Tell me what to do, Herr Flick.

FLICK. It is not right that the General should have the fifty thousand francs.

HELGA. Can you not order him to give it to you? How can anyone refuse you?

FLICK. Normally never! There is nowhere the Gestapo can't go!

HELGA. You don't need to tell me that!

FLICK. But in this case, the General seems to have friends in high places so I want you to go to him and steal it.

HELGA. Me, Herr Flick?

FLICK. Yes you. Use your feminine wiles…both of them…to seduce him and while he is distracted take the money. He has already indicated to me that he considers you a great piece of crackling.

HELGA. Oh, Herr Flick, do you really think I can pull it off?

FLICK. You have read my thoughts exactly!

HELGA. Very well Herr Flick. But I will not enjoy it!

FLICK. Then we can elope together. The sooner I get away the better. My superiors expect me to find the British airmen, but I fear that I will never catch them. Only this morning I received an urgent message tipping me off that the airmen would be in the town square at noon today.

HELGA. But why didn't you catch them then? That was over seven hours ago.

FLICK. The message was tied to a brick and thrown at my head. I have only just regained consciousness.

HELGA. Who would have the temerity to do such a wicked deed?

FLICK. Someone who hates me.

HELGA. Everybody hates you. Perhaps you should take reprisals.

FLICK. You cannot expect me to shoot everyone in the town. I'm unpopular enough as it is!

(Blackout.)

Scene Five
The Château

*(Later that night. The **GENERAL**'s dressing room in the château. There is a chair, table, small safe on the floor and a wardrobe. There are two doors/entrances. The main entrance and one leading to his bedroom. **KLINKERHOFFEN** is sitting in the chair comfortably, holding the cheese with the cash. For the ease of following the props, we will call this 'cheese#1'. He takes it to the safe and puts it in. He then takes out a cigar and contemplates lighting it.)*

GENERAL. Ah, life is good today. I have exactly what I want. I think I shall slip into something casual before a cigar and a little drinkie. Could life get any better? *(He opens his wardrobe but before he can do anything, there is a knock on the door.)* Come in.

*(**YVETTE** enters with a bottle of French brandy in one hand and the fake money cheese behind her back (cheese #2). She wiggles seductively in front of him.)*

Just when you think it can't, it does. Hello, my dear and what can I do for you?

YVETTE. I think General, it is more, what I can do for you. To get us in the mood I have bought along a bottle of fine French brandy. It is the best. Have a look at it.

*(The **GENERAL** takes the bottle and looks at it, and while he does so, **YVETTE** slides the cheese #2 under the table. The **GENERAL** puts the brandy on the table.)*

GENERAL. Well, never mind the brandy. We'll have it later. Perhaps some romantic music?

*(The **GENERAL** moves to the gramophone and puts on some quite unromantic music*. Sound effects: German Marching Music. The **GENERAL** starts to attempt to strip seductively to it. He takes off his jacket and attempts a stripper type movement, gyrating the jacket around his head before flinging it into the corner. He flings off his braces on his trousers. He then kicks off his shoes and hops around trying to take his socks off seductively. He manages to get one sock off and gyrates it around his head. **YVETTE** looks on in horror, when suddenly there is another knock at the door. **YVETTE** flings herself under the table. **KLINKERHOFFEN** rushes to pick up his jacket, puts it on and goes to the door, still holding a sock in one hand looking dishevelled. He opens the door and **HELGA** enters. She is wearing an officer's trench coat which she removes to reveal she is wearing very little underneath!)*

HELGA. Well, General, you look as if you are ready for me.

GENERAL. Ah, no, no. Um, one of my feet got hot you see… *(His trousers fall down, due to lack of braces.)*

HELGA. Oh General, you sexy beast you! Do not tell me that you don't yearn for me, with this romantic music playing.

GENERAL. What, you as well?

HELGA. What do you mean, you as well? I hope you are not being unfaithful as I have hoped that you were for me, and me alone.

---

* A license to produce 'Allo 'Allo 2 does not include a performance license for any third-party or copyrighted music. Licensees should create an original composition or use music in the public domain. For further information, please see the Music and Third-Party Materials Use Note on page iii.

GENERAL. I can't believe that this is happening. Maybe it's a dream. Helga, would you pinch me…hard.

HELGA. Ah, so that is what you are into. I have the whip. Let us go into the bedroom.

> *(**HELGA** leads him into his bedroom [off stage] with him hopping due to his trousers being down. **YVETTE** looks out from under the desk and comes out, leaving cheese #2 under the table.)*

YVETTE. Now, where is the other cheese?

> *(**YVETTE** starts searching but before she gets far, the door opens and **HERR FLICK**'s head appears around the door. **YVETTE** gets into the wardrobe. **HERR FLICK** comes in and looks around. He carries a picture frame.)*

FLICK. Ha, I shall check that Helga is not enjoying herself. I shall disguise myself as an oil painting of the Fuhrer himself.

> *(**HERR FLICK** puts on a silly moustache and wig and lifts the picture frame up to his face and stands in the corner. As he has just got into place there is a quiet knocking on the door, and **GRUBER** pokes his head in and looks around. He comes in. He is wearing a dressing gown.)*

GRUBER. What ghastly music. What else has he got? *(He goes to gramophone and looks at the records.).* Ah 'Love is the sweetest thing'. Much better. *(He puts this record on Sound effects: A popular jazz song plays*. As it starts,*

---

* A license to produce '*Allo 'Allo 2* does not include a performance license for any third-party or copyrighted music. Licensees should create an original composition or use music in the public domain. For further information, please see the Music and Third-Party Materials Use Note on page iii.

he picks up the brandy, looks at it and dances with it to the music. The music plays softly in background.)

Ah, Al Bowlly, I know you were British but…ooh so pretty.

> (**HERR FLICK** *makes a strangulated noise from his frame.)*

What was that? Hello? Hello? Who is there? Ah, just a figment of my imagination. Now what was I here for? Oh yes, the money.

> (**GRUBER** *starts to search and is looking under the table just as* **RENÉ**'s *head pops round the door and* **GRUBER** *quickly hides under said table, where he sees the cheese #2 and grabs it.* **RENÉ** *enters.)*

RENÉ. They cannot blow this place up. The recrimination will be terrible. And I do not want my little piece Yvette in little pieces! Yvette must be in with the General now, so it is safe for me to have a look around.

> *(Sound effects: There is a swish of a whip and a scream from off stage. Music is still playing quietly.)*

Dear me. Well, no matter if I am a quick, I can find both cheeses, switch the money, and retrieve the bomb. Ah, a safe.

> (**RENÉ** *finds the safe and bends over to open it. As he is fiddling with it, bent over,* **GRUBER** *creeps out from under the table and up behind him holding his cheese #2, and coughs discreetly.* **RENÉ** *looks round without standing up.)*

Oh, hello Lieutenant Gruber. You find me in a difficult position…

GRUBER. Well, René, I'm not grumbling as you can see...

RENÉ. Let me explain...

GRUBER. I think that explanations are not required under these circumstances.

RENÉ. Well, Lieutenant...

GRUBER. René...call me... Hubert. Tell me René, that you could find it in your heart...

> (**RENÉ** *looks back into the safe and sees the camembert – cheese #1.*)

RENÉ. I have found it... I have found it...

GRUBER. Oh René, I knew it, I knew it.

> (**RENÉ** *stands up with the cheese #1 and* **GRUBER** *grabs him, turns him around and they dance with* **RENÉ** *not quite knowing what to do.* **GRUBER** *is still holding cheese #2.*)

Ah, the music, the romance, the smell of cheese...

RENÉ. *(Noticing the 'portrait' of Hitler.)* The portrait of Hitler...

GRUBER. *(Studying it too.)* Yes, it is most realistic. I feel almost as if he were watching us. Very clever usage of linear perspective don't you think.

RENÉ. Oh yes, I have spent hours pondering on it. You seem to know a lot about paintings?

GRUBER. Back in Munich before the war, I was an artist in a gallery. I used to touch up the old masters.

RENÉ. Why am I not surprised?

GRUBER. Oh René, I wish that this moment would last forever, us together at last, dancing cheek to cheek, discussing art, with our own personal cheeses...

> (**YVETTE** *bursts from the wardrobe.* **RENÉ** *and* **GRUBER** *both drop their cheeses in shock.* **YVETTE** *turns off the gramophone music.* **RENÉ** *is in a panic staring at the cheeses as he is worried that the bomb may go off.*)

YVETTE. Oh René, are you all right?

RENÉ. All the better for seeing you, Yvette!

GRUBER. René. I am very disappointed. You must make a decision. What do you want to do with your life?

RENÉ. To be truthful all I am looking for is happiness.

GRUBER. Well, yes, me too, but a long-term relationship would be nice.

YVETTE. Listen, both of you, we have no time for this. Now which camembert is which?

RENÉ. I don't know. But be very careful with them!

GRUBER. Whatever is the matter?

RENÉ. Lieutenant, can I trust you…?

YVETTE. Oh, René, be careful what you say. Walls have ears you know.

RENÉ. Oh don't be so dramatic girl, there are only the three of us here.

> (*The* **GENERAL** *bursts in, wearing only his vest and underpants. They all stop and look at one another.*)

… Well, four of us…

GRUBER. Oooh, General…

> (**HELGA** *enters with a whip.*)

RENÉ. … Well, five then…

> (**HERR FLICK** *drops his frame over his head.*)

FLICK. Helga, how dare you enjoy yourself!

GENERAL & GRUBER. Heil Hitler!

GENERAL. How embarrassing and me in my shreddies.

RENÉ. Six...

> (**FLICK** *chases* **HELGA** *off stage into the bedroom, followed by the* **GENERAL**.*)*

GRUBER. You know René, I thought that painting was too realistic.

RENÉ. Never mind all that. We have to get out of here... and be careful with the cheeses!

GRUBER. You are right. We do not wish to squish them!

RENÉ. *(Aside to* **YVETTE**.*)* There is a bomb in one of them!

YVETTE. A bo...?

RENÉ. *(Aside to* **YVETTE**.*)* Shhhh!

> (**RENÉ** *looks at them both and identifies cheese #2.)*

Ah this is the one. Hold this, Lieutenant.

> (**RENÉ** *hands cheese #2 to* **GRUBER**. **HERR FLICK** *returns from the bedroom.)*

GRUBER. *(Giving the salute and throwing cheese #2 into the air.)* Heil Hitler!

YVETTE. René, catch it!

> (**RENÉ** *catches cheese #2 ...just. He throws it rugby style to* **YVETTE** *who catches it.)*

RENÉ. Now go Yvette.

> (**YVETTE** *makes a rapid exit.)*

FLICK. I am not the Fuhrer!

RENÉ. Surely it is not Leclerc in his first believable disguise.

FLICK. No, it is I, Herr Flick, and you may be assured that the Fuhrer will hear about this and you will all be shot.

*(The **GENERAL**, still in his vest and underpants, enters having heard all this.)*

GENERAL. Herr Flick, do you know the punishment for impersonating the Fuhrer?

FLICK. But General, I have information…

GENERAL. Go Herr Flick and I will take no more action. Take this dangerous woman with you. I have had enough of her…for tonight.

*(**HERR FLICK** and **HELGA** exit.)*

I shall go and put something on and then I shall deal with you two.

*(The **GENERAL** goes off stage.)*

GRUBER. René, quick you must go.

RENÉ. But what about the General?

GRUBER. Leave him to me!

*(**RENÉ** dashes off through the door. **GRUBER**, remembering his mission picks up cheese #1 and looks about to see where he could hide it. He pushes it up the back of his jacket just as the **GENERAL** comes back in wearing a dressing gown.)*

GENERAL. Right then. What are you doing here Gruber? Where is that peasant? *(He notices **GRUBER**'s stoop!)* And what is wrong with you?

GRUBER. I heard a disturbance General and popped in to check you were alright.

(The **GENERAL** *stares at* **GRUBER**'*s back some more.)*

Ah well, you see General, as you know I am bit of a thespian, and I have just been cast in a local production of the 'Hunchback of Notre Dame'. And um, I'm just on my way to a rehearsal.

GENERAL. Oh, I see. Well, you'd better be on your way then. And do not disturb me again!

GRUBER. Thank you sir. Um, let me see, yes, the Bells, the Bells…

*(***GRUBER** *exits through the door.)*

GENERAL. What a strange evening. Well, at least my money is safe. *(He goes to the safe and opens it. He reacts.)* WHAT? I have been burgled! GUARDS!!!

(Blackout.)

Scene Six
Fanny's Bedroom

(**FANNY** *is asleep in her bedroom.* **LECLERC** *is also in the bed, unseen under the covers.* **RENÉ** *and* **EDITH** *enter followed by* **CRABTREE** *and* **MICHELLE**.)

FANNY. *(Woken by the sound.)* Aaaahhh! Who is this in my room?

RENÉ. Shut up you silly old bat. It is only us.

EDITH. Sorry Mama.

FANNY. Why must you disturb me so late at night?

RENÉ. Ask her… *(He points at* **MICHELLE**.*)*

MICHELLE. Now listen very carefully, I shall say this only once.

FANNY. What was that?

MICHELLE. I shall say this only once.

FANNY. Good.

MICHELLE. Our latest plan to catapult the airmen back to England has failed.

RENÉ. There's a surprise.

CRABTREE. The elastic bond snipped.

MICHELLE. We need to call London to tell them the bad news.

RENÉ. I wish you would leave us in peace and stop these stupid schemes. I have only just got back from the château with the forged money and your bomb. What were you thinking of, trying to blow up the General?

FANNY. *(To* **EDITH**.*)* Why have I been left alone so long?

LECLERC. *(Sitting up in the bed next to **FANNY**.)* I had a headache.

EDITH. What is Monsieur Leclerc doing in your bed?

FANNY. He was sleeping in the cellar, and I felt sorry for him. It is very windy down there.

LECLERC. It is not much better up here.

FANNY. Am I not allowed a little romance and attention?

RENÉ. I'm surprised you'd get any from him.

EDITH. My mother and Leclerc…it is very romantic!

RENÉ. It is certainly rheumatic. Come on let's get this over with quickly.

> *(**RENÉ**, **EDITH**, **CRABTREE** and **MICHELLE** lift up the bed to set up the **RADIO**.)*

LECLERC. I hope this does not happen on the honeymoon!

FANNY. Why not? Nothing else will happen.

RENÉ. *(To the **RADIO**.)* 'Allo 'allo! This is Nighthawk. Can you hear me? Can you hear me? Over.

FANNY. *(Holding her ear trumpet to her ear and interrupting.)* Of course I can hear you.

RENÉ. Not you! Shut up!

RADIO. *(In a French accent.)* 'Allo Nighthawk. Are you receiving us? Over?

RENÉ. *(To the **RADIO**.)* Receiving you loud and crackling. Over.

RADIO. Pass your message. Over.

RENÉ. *(To **EDITH**.)* What is the code to tell them the British airmen are still here?

EDITH. *(Reading from the code book.)* "The little cupboard is full."

FANNY. Ah? What is that?

RENÉ. *(To the **RADIO**.)* The little cupboard is full! Over.

FANNY. *(Interrupting again.)* Oh no, no, no. I have not used it all the day!

RADIO. Understood. Philip and John are going for a swim. Heloise is expecting a visit from the stork. Over.

RENÉ. *(To **EDITH**.)* What is that supposed to mean?

CRABTREE. Leave it to moo. *(Into the **RADIO**.)* 'Allo 'Allo, secret agent Crabtree cooling. Give me Wombledon sox two, sox two

RADIO. Receiving you lewd and clore. Hold the loon, I will connoct you.

RENÉ. Not another one!

RADIO 2. *(A very English voice.)* Hello. Johnson's tailors. How can I help you?

CRABTREE. *(He breaks the connection.)* Bigger. A wrong nimber. I will go and chick it in my address bike.

MICHELLE. We will return soon!

RENÉ. Oh, good…

>   *(**CRABTREE** and **MICHELLE** exit out of the window.)*

MIMI. *(Off stage.)* Stop! You cannot go in there!

>   *(**GRUBER** enters with **MIMI** close behind. **GRUBER** carries a camembert cheese.)*

I could not stop him!

GRUBER. Good evening, everyone.

FANNY. A German in my bedroom! They rape defenceless women!

MIMI. Believe me, this one doesn't.

LECLERC. I will protect you, Fanny!

FANNY. Do your worst! I am prepared to die for France. I have been prepared for thirty years.

RENÉ. God clearly doesn't want the aggravation. *(To* **GRUBER.***)* What are you doing here Lieutenant?

GRUBER. I am sorry to intrude René, but I have something for you...

RENÉ. Something for me Lieutenant?

GRUBER. Yes, here. I stole this from the General.

> *(**GRUBER** hands over the cheese to **RENÉ**, who looks inside.)*

RENÉ. But it is empty?

GRUBER. Ah, the money is safe...

> *(**GRUBER** starts to unbutton his trousers.)*

FANNY. Aaaaaahhhhh!

RENÉ. Lieutenant!

> *(**GRUBER** reveals the money tucked into his undergarments.)*

GRUBER. I have a large package for you...

FANNY & EDITH. Aaaaaahhhhh!

GRUBER. I was under orders to bring the money back to the Colonel, but I think you need it more than he does...

> *(**GRUBER** hands the bundles of cash to **RENÉ**.)*

EDITH. But now we have both...

RENÉ. *(Interrupting her quickly.)* Thank you, Edith. Lieutenant, how can I ever thank you.

GRUBER. Oh I'm sure I'll think of something. Good night then.

(**GRUBER** *exits escorted by* **MIMI**.)

RENÉ. Why are people always trying to help me! Now we are back to square one!

(**MICHELLE** *appears at the window and opens it. She does not come in but peers through.*)

Will you get down from there?

EDITH. Someone will see you!

MICHELLE. If I am seen I will simply say I am repairing your window.

RENÉ. But it is not broken!

(**MICHELLE** *hits the window. Sound effects: Broken glass.*)

MICHELLE. It is now.

RENÉ. Oh, thank you. You realise now that the general does not have either cheese and therefore no money and no doubt, he will come here tomorrow to get it back.

MICHELLE. He may have you shot.

RENÉ. He can join the queue. The undertaker with the dicky ticker is already coming to shoot me.

MICHELLE. The resistance will protect you. Without your help the British airmen will never get home. If necessary, we will shoot you first.

RENÉ. What!

MICHELLE. Do not worry, we will fake your death so you will be left alone. (*Pause.*) But if the plan fails…

RENÉ. And of course, your track record is *so* good…

MICHELLE. ...The Germans may arrest you and we would not want you to suffer.

LECLERC. They do not want you to talk!

MICHELLE. Here is a suicide pill hidden in this ring.

(**MICHELLE** *hands* **RENÉ** *a ring.*)

RENÉ. Oh Michelle, no thank you, I just want a quiet life.

EDITH. Take the pill and you'll have one!

MICHELLE. Perhaps you would like to give your wife one?

RENÉ. Even a Frenchman cannot think of that sort of thing at a time like this.

MICHELLE. I will now depart like a phantom into the night...

(**MICHELLE** *exits through the window.*)

RENÉ. Well, she was a great help!

(*Sound effects: Clatter, pause and a crash.*)

EDITH. What was that?

RENÉ. Just the phantom falling off the roof! Come let us prepare for tomorrow.

EDITH. If this is to be your last night alive, we will make it a night to remember. Let me do something that will make you feel warm and wonderful!

RENÉ. Good idea. You can fill my hot water bottle.

(*Blackout.*)

Scene Seven
René's Café

*(The next day in the café. Peasants and Germans are gathered at the tables anticipating events. **RENÉ** is in a fluster. **YVETTE** and **MIMI** are on hand to support him.)*

RENÉ. Well, I tell you this, it is not good to ponder on the fact that this may be the last day of my life although I suppose things would be somewhat less fraught, and truth to tell, I could do with a lie down. Both the General and the undertaker want the money and I cannot pay them both.

MIMI. Oh, René, I will defend you from death…

YVETTE. Oh, René, I will defend you from death even more…

RENÉ. How can you defend me even more from death?

MIMI. We have a plan René. I have a gun here under my apron and it is loaded with blank bullets, and I will shoot you. When I do, please scream and clutch your chest.

YVETTE. And I will rush to you, and you will collapse on top of me, which will allow me to apply some false blood to your body without being seen, while under the pretence of giving you the kiss of life.

MIMI. And then I will lift your body off and we shall wail.

YVETTE. The General will see you are dead with blood all over you. We will do some more weeping and then carry your body out the back, shove you down into the coal cellar and all will be well.

RENÉ. Well, I suppose it's the thought that counts and maybe it will work.

*(The **COLONEL** and **GEERING** enter through the main door.)*

COLONEL. René?

RENÉ. Yes Colonel?

COLONEL. We are here to warn you that the General is on the warpath. If you don't give him his money, he will kill you. Now René, I shall be frank with you. We don't want that.

RENÉ. I'm touched, Colonel, that true friendship can cross the boundaries of nationality.

COLONEL. We are concerned René that if you were to die, then the new owners would put up the prices…

GEERING. …And the girls may be of a lesser quality.

RENÉ. Oh charming. So, what are we to do?

GEERING. Well René, we have a plan. The Colonel has a gun, loaded with blank bullets, and he will shoot you. You must scream and clutch your chest, whereupon I will rush to you. You will collapse on top of me allowing me to apply some false blood with no-one seeing me do it. We will drag you out the back and throw you down into the coal cellar.

RENÉ. I see. What a unique idea? Some wine perhaps while we are waiting?

*(**RENÉ** beckons **YVETTE** and **MIMI** to attend to the officers. **MICHELLE** enters through the main door and beckons **RENÉ** over to her.)*

MICHELLE. René, listen very carefully, I shall say this only once.

RENÉ. Well in that case speak very slowly! What are you doing here and where are those wretched airmen now?

MICHELLE. They are safely away. They are finally gone. We have posted them to Switzerland.

RENÉ. Posted them!?

MICHELLE. Yes, in large boxes. You need worry no more about them.

RENÉ. Well, that is one thing out of the way I suppose but I am still in a predicament.

MICHELLE. I have a plan. Under my coat I have a gun which is loaded with blank bullets. I will shoot you and when I do, you must scream and clutch your chest.

RENÉ. Don't tell me, you will rush towards me, I will fall on you while you apply some fake blood, and you will drag me out and throw me down the coal cellar?

MICHELLE. How did you know that? It's classified information!

RENÉ. It was an inspired guess.

> (**HERR FLICK** and **HELGA** enter through the main doors. **MICHELLE** moves away. **HERR FLICK** and **HELGA** approach **RENÉ**.)

Herr Flick, what a pleasant surprise?

FLICK. René, I am here to shoot you.

RENÉ. What?

FLICK. I know what the General intends but no-one can cross the Gestapo and get away with it. I will shoot you first but, here is the twist, it will be with blank bullets. You will scream and clutch your chest at which point Helga will rush to you.

HELGA. I will apply false blood as you fall on me. We will then carry you outside and deposit you in the coal cellar.

FLICK. Against my instincts I will save you, but with a condition. You will then tell me where the British airmen are? Is this an agreement?

RENÉ. *(To audience.)* Well, why not? They'll be in Switzerland. *(Turning to* **FLICK**.*)* I agree Herr Flick.

> *(***HERR FLICK*** and ***HELGA*** *go and sit down.* ***EDITH*** *enters down the stairs.* ***RENÉ*** *crosses to her.)*

EDITH. René, I have something dangerous under my skirt.

RENÉ. I imagine you have...

EDITH. Quiet. I thought I should warn you that I am going to pretend to kill you. I have a gun.

RENÉ. Does this plan end with me in the coal cellar?

EDITH. Yes, it does.

RENÉ. Well, don't bother to explain. I'll improvise.

> *(The* ***GENERAL*** *and* ***GRUBER*** *enter through the main door. Rene hides behind the bar.)*

GENERAL. Heil Hitler!

GERMANS. Heil Hitler!

GEERING. *(Late.)* 'Tler!

GENERAL. Where is the cafe owner? I have had enough of this nonsense and now I shall shoot him.

EDITH. Perhaps a glass of wine first?

> *(***EDITH***,* ***MIMI*** *and* ***YVETTE*** *busy themselves around the* ***GENERAL*** *and attempt to ply him with a glass of wine.* ***MICHELLE*** *approaches* ***GRUBER***.*)*

MICHELLE. You do not want René to die do you?

GRUBER. No, no, I don't.

MICHELLE. Then listen to me. We can save him. Take this gun with blank bullets and shoot him. I will rush to him, and he will collapse on top of me...

GRUBER. Maybe you could shoot him, and he could fall on top of me?

MICHELLE. No, no, no. I have it worked out. He will fall on me, and I will apply false blood on his chest as we fall.

GRUBER. Well, yes, and then what?

MICHELLE. You will pull him off...

*(**GRUBER** reacts.)*

... Thus allowing everyone to see he is dead.

GRUBER. *(Slightly disappointed.)* Oh yes, I see.

MICHELLE. We then take him to the coal cellar, and all will be well.

*(The **GENERAL** by this time has pushed away the girls and has approached the bar. He looks over the bar.)*

GENERAL. Come out from behind there!

*(**RENÉ** stands up with his hands held high. The **GENERAL** pulls out his pistol.)*

I will give you thirty seconds to make peace with yourself and then I shall kill you.

RENÉ. Thank you.

*(**FANNY** appears on the stairs with a shotgun.)*

FANNY. ...Aha, at last I can have my revenge!

RENÉ. Why do *you* want to kill me?

FANNY. I just don't like you.

RENÉ. Anyone else?

> *(Everyone on the stage pull out guns and aim them at* **RENÉ**. **MONSIEUR ALPHONSE** *enters through the main door carrying a duelling pistol.)*

ALPHONSE. Stop!

> *(Everyone freezes.)*

(To **RENÉ**.*)* You bounder. I have our duelling pistols and we shall fight to the death.

> *(At this point everyone is standing ready to kill* **RENÉ**. **RENÉ** *steps forward.)*

RENÉ. No, no, no, no. *(Pause.)* I give in. I am all done. Can I propose a way forward here?

ALL. What?

GEERING. *(Late.)* What?

RENÉ. I just give you the money and we all go about our business as normal. Edith? Give him the money *(Aside to* **EDITH**.*)* The real money.

> *(***EDITH** *quickly exits to the back room to collect a camembert.)*

GENERAL. You have the money?

RENÉ. Yes, yes.

> *(Everyone relaxes.* **EDITH** *returns with the cheese.)*

EDITH. It is all there General.

GENERAL. Well, that's good. Everyone is happy. Especially me. Well, Gruber, please take me back to the château. In your little tank.

GRUBER. Certainly General.

*(All the **GERMANS** leave. **FANNY** goes back up stairs.)*

RENÉ. Well, that is that. I am at least alive but we have lost the money.

*(**LECLERC** enters from the back room. He carries a camembert.)*

LECLERC. It is I, Leclerc.

RENÉ. Who are you disguised as now?

LECLERC. I am disguised as Leclerc today. It is a new ploy.

RENÉ. It is very good, possibly your best disguise.

LECLERC. I have the cheese.

*(**LECLERC** hands the cheese to **RENÉ**.)*

RENÉ. Oh yes, we had better get this wretched bomb defused. It could go off at any time.

MICHELLE. No, it is perfectly safe now.

LECLERC. The bomb will not go off unless the detonator pin is removed.

YVETTE. That is very clever.

*(**RENÉ** opens the cheese up and looks at the notes.)*

RENÉ. These notes look very good actually, better than I remember. They could almost be real.

MICHELLE. There is no bomb in here René.

ALPHONSE. Oh excellent, my money back.

RENÉ. No, no, wait a minute. If we have the real money, happy though we may be, then the fake money with the bomb must be…

FANNY. *(Appearing on the stairs.)* Roger? What is this thing that you have left in my under sheets? It has been poking me dreadfully.

LECLERC. It is nothing, Fanny. Just a detonator pin.

> *(They freeze and look at each other. There is three seconds silence, and then... sound effects: Huge explosion off stage. A little tank exploding! There is a cloud of smoke and a shower of bank notes through the main door. There is short, shocked pause.* **GRUBER** *enters, covered in soot, in torn clothes, with a steering wheel around his neck.)*

GRUBER. My little tank!

> *(All the other* **GERMANS** *come back in through the main door, also sooted up and looking somewhat dishevelled!)*

GENERAL. My money, Gruber you fool, my money!

GRUBER. It is not my fault Herr General, I let Field Marshal Rommel borrow my tank yesterday, and he assured me that he would service it fully. He must have forgotten so perhaps you should take it up with the Field Marshal. If he's a reasonable man, surely he will recompense you?

> *(The* **GENERAL** *looks stunned.)*

Or maybe not.

COLONEL. You cannot blame it on us this time. We were not responsible…

GEERING. I was totally irresponsible.

GENERAL. We will discuss this back at the Château. Come!

> *(The* **GENERAL**, **COLONEL**, **GEERING** *and* **GRUBER** *exit through the main door.)*

FLICK. *(To* **HELGA***.)* This is an unfortunate but satisfactory result.

HELGA. But we do not have the money Herr Flick.

FLICK. And neither does the General. We must return to Gestapo Headquarters immediately where I intend to debrief you thoroughly.

HELGA. *(Enthusiastically.)* At once Herr Flick.

> *(***HERR FLICK** *and* **HELGA** *exit through the main door.)*

MICHELLE. I will now disappear like a...

RENÉ. Yes, yes, go away and take this idiot *(Indicating* **LECLERC***.)* with you. Oh, and Michelle, please do not involve me in any more of your plans for the foreseeable future! Like the next five years, go...go!

> *(***RENÉ** *chivvies* **MICHELLE** *and* **LECLERC** *out of the main door and looks out on the square outside.)*

Oh, look at the mess. Mimi, Yvette, you had better go outside and help clear up the square. We don't want to put off the customers.

> *(***MIMI** *and* **YVETTE** *take brooms from behind the bar and exit through the main door to start clearing.* **RENÉ**, **EDITH** *and* **MONSIEUR ALPHONSE** *are left alone.)*

ALPHONSE. Well, as they say, all's well that ends well.

RENÉ. I must admit that it could have been worse. Here is your money Monsieur Alphonse.

> *(***RENÉ** *starts handing bundles of money out of the cheese back to* **ALPHONSE**. **ALPHONSE** *holds each bundle to his ear and quickly*

FLICKS through it, mentally counting it. After all the bundles are counted...)

ALPHONSE. This is five hundred francs short René.

RENÉ. How can you tell?

ALPHONSE. Experience.

*(**RENÉ** delves into the cheese again and pulls out the last note.)*

RENÉ. Here!

*(**RENÉ** hands the note to **ALPHONSE**. **ALPHONSE** looks lovingly at **EDITH**.)*

ALPHONSE. Madam. I have decided that, given the circumstances, not only will I waive the interest, but if René promises to spend the money wisely, on something for you, then you can keep the five hundred francs.

EDITH. Oh, Monsieur Alphonse. How can I ever thank you?

ALPHONSE. Oh, I'm sure something will come up.

*(**RENÉ** ushers **ALPHONSE** out the main door, thanking him. **EDITH** and **RENÉ** are left alone.)*

EDITH. Oh René. At last, we have all we want.

RENÉ. Yes.

EDITH. We have five hundred francs which we weren't expecting.

RENÉ. Yes.

EDITH. And we are, at last, alone.

RENÉ. Well, you can't have everything I suppose...

*(**CRABTREE** enters through the main door.)*

CRABTREE. Good moaning.

RENÉ. Oh, what do you want?

CRABTREE. I am covering for the Pistman who is in bed with the flea. You sent a pockage with incorrect stimps. I've come to collect the outstinding pooment. *(He waves a paper invoice.)*

RENÉ. Oh no, that idiot Michelle. How much is it?

CRABTREE. Five hundred froncs.

> *(**RENÉ** hands over the money sadly. **CRABTREE** takes it and starts moving to the door.)*

RENÉ. Ah well, a price worth paying. The packages were delivered safely I assume Mr Pistman.

> *(**CRABTREE** ushers in two members of the chorus who are pushing sack barrows on which are two large [wardrobe packing box sized] cardboard boxes.)*

CRABTREE. No Ronnie. Return to sinder.

> *(**CRABTREE** and the delivery men exit through the main door leaving the boxes.)*

EDITH. What are these René?

> *(**RENÉ** has retreated in despair behind the bar and pours himself a very large drink.)*

René?

> *(**RENÉ** now has his head in his hands. **EDITH** is peering closely at the boxes. The **BRITISH AIRMEN** burst out of the boxes waving Union Jack flags and looking excited.)*

BRITISH AIRMEN. HELLO!

(They then realise where they are and react. General reaction and blackout. Curtain. Sound effects:" 'Allo 'Allo" theme music.* Blackout.)

---

* A licence to produce *'Allo 'Allo 2* does not include a performance licence for "'Allo 'Allo theme music". The publisher and author suggest that the licensee contact PRS to ascertain the music publisher and contact such music publisher to license or acquire permission for performance of the song. If a licence or permission is unattainable for "'Allo 'Allo theme music", the licensee may not use the song in *'Allo 'Allo 2* but should create an original composition in a similar style or use a similar song in the public domain. For further information, please see the Music and Third-Party Materials Use Note on page iii.

STAGING NOTES

The size of your stage / venue and the resources you have available to you will dictate how you choose to set the scenes.

Rene's Café is key to the show and requires suitable space for the action including tables, chairs and a bar top.

The simpler settings of Herr Flick's Dungeon and the Colonel's HQ can be done as interchangeable 'front of cloth' scenes or be set to one side / in front of the stage.

Likewise the funeral parlour and the railway station can be staged simply to the front or side of the main set. The château scene can have its own set or could be staged on the café area with some appropriate redressing and addition of the correct furniture.

In the original production, with a wide stage and expansive side aprons, the set was built (Stage right to stage left) as follows. Herr Flick's Dungeon on the SR apron, a town square space (exterior of the café) covering half of the stage that was used as the railway station, Alphonse's parlour with additional signage, and converted to become the château room. The other half of the stage was used for René's Café with a raised section behind it that was used as Fanny's bedroom. The SL apron was used for the Colonel's HQ. Further action spilled on the area in front of the stage (e.g. the can-can dance).

The following diagrams give a suggestion on how the staging can work.

ACT ONE STAGING SUGGESTION

ACT TWO STAGING SUGGESTION

PROPS LIST

This list includes all named/mentioned items from the script.

In addition, you will require set dressing items – in particular, in the café (table cloths, trays, bottles, glasses, cruet sets, baskets etc.) which the cast can use/interact with.

Act	Scene	Item	Personal/Set on stage	OK
1	1	Cleaning cloth	On bar	
1	1	Drinking Glasses	On bar	
1	1	Wine bottle	Table	
1	1	4 × wine glasses	Table	
1	1	Bag of groceries	Edith	
1	2	Military Map	Wall	
1	2	Manila folder	Colonel	
1	2	'Reichstags and Reichhens' magazine	Colonel	
1	2	Long wooden pointer	By Wall	
1	3	Ear Trumpet	Fanny	
1	3	Bowl of soup and a spoon	Edith	
1	3	Knitting	Side table	
1	3	Radio (inc. Microphone on wire)	Under bed	
1	4	Playing cards	Helga and Flick	
1	4	Pen and pencil set	Desk	
1	4	Telephone	Desk	
1	4	Gramophone (*optional*)	Table	
1	4	Box of needles	Desk or Flick	

1	5	Wine glasses and Bottle	Bar	
1	5	Cognac glass and bottle	Bar	
1	5	Wrench/spanner	Michelle	
1	6	Tape measure	Alphonse	
1	6	Bank notes	Alphonse	
1	6	2 × spoons	Alphonse	
1	6	Contract and pen	Table	
1	7	Cleaning cloth	Bar	
1	7	2 × Flying helmets	Mimi and Yvette	
1	7	Cash	German Soldier	
1	7	Cash	Till	
1	7	Tray with 4 × champagne (saucer/cup style) glasses and 2 × bottle of Champagne	Bar	
1	7	Cheese pieces (yellow foam)	Colonel and Geering	
1	7	2 × Strings of Onions	Flick	
1	7	1 × string of Onions	Helga	
1	7	Bag (containing his hat)	Flick	
1	7	Selection of cheeses	Leclerc	
1	7	False camembert with money	Leclerc	
1	7	Pistol	General	
2	1	Gloves	Alphonse	
2	1	Shopping bag with groceries	Yvette	
2	1	Notepapers and pen	Bar	
2	1	Brown envelope	Bar	
2	1	White envelope	Bar	

2	2	***None***		
2	3	Suitcase	René	
2	3	Suitcase	Edith	
2	3	Policeman's whistle	Crabtree	
2	3	Mountaineering gear	LeClerc	
2	3	2nd False camembert, containing cash	Leclerc	
2	4	Boiled egg and spoon	Desk/Flick	
2	4	Envelope containing invitation	Desk	
2	5	False camembert containing cash	General	
2	5	Cigar	General	
2	5	Safe	Set	
2	5	Bottle of Brandy	Yvette	
2	5	2nd False camembert, containing cash	Yvette	
2	5	Gramophone & records	Set	
2	5	Hitler Moustache	Flick	
2	5	Hitler Wig	Flick	
2	5	Picture frame surround	Flick	
2	5	Whip	Helga	
2	6	Ear Trumpet	Fanny	
2	6	Radio (inc. Microphone on wire)	Under bed	
2	6	Code book	Under bed with radio	
2	6	False camembert, containing cash	Gruber	
2	6	Suicide ring	Michelle	

2	7	Pistol	Mimi	
2	7	Pistol	Colonel	
2	7	Pistol	Flick	
2	7	Pistol	Michelle	
2	7	Pistol	Edith	
2	7	Wine bottle and glasses	Yvette	
2	7	Pistol	General	
2	7	Shotgun	Fanny	
2	7	False camembert, containing fake cash	Edith	
2	7	2nd False camembert, containing cash	Leclerc	
2	7	Detonator pin	Fanny	
2	7	Steering wheel	Gruber	
2	7	500 franc note	Inside cheese	
2	7	2 × Brooms	Mimi and Yvette	
2	7	Postal bill/invoice	Crabtree	
2	7	2 × sack trucks for packages	Chorus	
2	7	Duelling pistol	Alphonse	
2	7	2 x packing cases	British Airmen	

LIGHTING PLOT

ACT ONE

Scene One
To open:	Bring up lights on the café
Cue 1	René and Edith exit
	Fade lights to blackout

Scene Two
To open:	Bring up lights on the Colonel's HQ set
Cue 2	Gruber: 'Yes…yes…of course.'
	Fade lights to blackout

Scene Three
To open:	Bring up lights on the Fanny's bedroom
Cue 3	René: 'Be quiet will you, we are awaiting an urgent message from London.'
	Flashing bed knobs
Cue 4	René: 'Just what I was thinking.'
	Fade lights to blackout

Scene Four
To open:	Bring up lights on the Herr Flick's dungeon
Cue 5	Flick 'Played at double speed, he sounds like Donald Duck.'
	Fade lights to blackout

Scene Five
To open:	Bring up lights on the café
Cue 6	Edith 'And now I must practise. This little number will bring the house down.'
	Fade lights to blackout

Scene Six
To open:	Bring up lights on the funeral parlour
Cue 7	René and Edith exit. Fade out on a happy looking Alphonse clutching his contract.
	Fade lights to blackout

Scene Seven
To open:	Bring up lights on the Café
Cue 8	René snaps his fingers; everyone freezes.
	Spot on René with fade on others

Cue 9	René snaps his fingers; everyone unfreezes. Fade up on others
Cue 10	René: '...Why don't you pop off for a quick interval?' Fade lights to blackout

ACT TWO

Scene One

To open:	Bring up lights on the café
Cue 11	LeClerc: 'The one in the white for the bit of alright. Simple!' Fade lights to blackout

Scene Two

To open:	Bring up lights on the Colonel's HQ set
Cue 12	Geering: 'You'll need it...' Fade lights to blackout

Scene Three

To open:	Bring up lights on the Railway Station
Cue 13	René's exit after: '... I must go and stop Yvette and bring that cheese back before she gets hurt.' Fade lights to blackout

Scene Four

To open:	Bring up lights on the Herr Flick's dungeon
Cue 14	Flick 'You cannot expect me to shoot everyone in the town. I'm unpopular enough as it is!' Fade lights to blackout

Scene Five

To open:	Bring up lights on the General's dressing room at the château
Cue 15	General: '... WHAT? I have been burgled! GUARDS!!!' Fade lights to blackout

Scene Six

To open:	Bring up lights on the Fanny's bedroom
Cue 16	René: 'Good idea. You can fill my hot water bottle.' Fade lights to blackout

Scene Seven

To open:	Bring up lights on the café
Cue 17	LeClerc: 'It is nothing, Fanny. Just a detonator pin!'

Cue 18　　Flashing light FX for explosion synced with sound FX
　　　　　British Airmen: HELLO!
　　　　　After line with pause for general effect and cast reaction
　　　　　Fade lights to blackout

EFFECTS PLOT

You may also want to use short musical stings to cover the changes of scenes. Please see music note on Piii.

ACT ONE

Scene One

Cue 1 — On start of show
"*'Allo 'Allo*" theme music

Scene Two

None required

Scene Three

Cue 2 — René: 'Be quiet will you, we are awaiting an urgent message from London.'
Buzzing tone in sync with flashing lights lighting effect on bedstead

Cue 3 — Fanny: 'Oh my knitting, my stitching!'
fart effect

Cue 4 — René: 'A weak and ill old lady when it suits her.'
Radio static/whistling

Scene Four

Cue 5 — Helga: 'I'm telling the truth, Herr Flick.'
Telephone

Scene Five

None required

Scene Six

None required

Scene Seven

Cue 6 — Edith '... I will start with a little musical number...'
Your choice of musical track for Edith to sing along to

Cue 7 — Edith 'And now for your delight; the can-can girls of Nancy!
Can-Can music

Cue 8 — René: '... Why don't you pop off for a quick interval?'
"*'Allo 'Allo*" theme music to play out

ACT TWO

Scene One

Cue 9   On start of Act Two
'*Allo 'Allo'* theme music

Scene Two

None required

Scene Three

Cue 10   On start of scene
Steam Train whistle and sounds

Cue 11   Carstairs: 'Yes, but I wish we hadn't had onion soup for tea!'
Loud fart effect

Scene Four

None required

Scene Five

Cue 12   General: 'Well, never mind the brandy. We'll have it later. Perhaps some romantic music?'
German martial marching music

Cue 13   Gruber: 'Ah 'Love is the sweetest thing'. Much better.'
'Love is the sweetest thing' – *A popular jazz song plays*

Cue 14   René: '... Yvette must be in with the General now, so it is safe for me to have a look around.'
Swish of whip and scream

Scene Six

Cue 15   René: 'But it is not broken!'
Breaking glass of window

Cue 16   René: 'Well, she was a great help!'
Clatter and crash

Scene Seven

Cue 17   LeClerc: 'It is nothing, Fanny. Just a detonator pin!'
Explosion effect
Smoke and shower of notes and assorted debris

Cue 18   British Airmen: HELLO!
After short pause for reactions
'*Allo 'Allo*' theme music to play out

ABOUT THE AUTHORS

David Croft is best known for writing sitcom hits such as *Dad's Army*, *Hi de Hi!*, *Ain't Half Hot Mum* and *You Rang M'Lord* with Jimmy Perry. David's 'hits' continued when he joined forces with Jeremy Lloyd, producing and writing shows such as *Are You Being Served?*, *'Allo 'Allo*, *Grace and Favour*, *Come Back Mrs Noah* and, *Oh Happy Band*.

It is difficult to say when Lloyd and Croft first met, but they were nodding acquaintances for many years, both writing sketches individually and parodies of songs for *The Billy Cotton Band Show*, in which Lloyd played again the British Public School idiot he was so loved for in America

Their paths crossed again when Croft was asked by Sir Bill Cotton to bring his expertise to help a programme by Jilly Cooper called *It's Awfully Bad for your Eyes Darling* (1971). Lloyd was playing a part in it – (another Public School idiot!). Croft & Lloyd collaborated to re-write the first five minutes of the show to give it a few more laughs but, alas they failed to save it. However, during this time Lloyd mentioned that he had an outline for a show based on his experiences in the men's department at Simpsons of Piccadilly. Croft liked the idea a lot, so they got together to write a show that became *Are You Being Served?* (1972-85). Their nodding acquaintance became a life-long friendship, a hilarious and prolific partnership that also produced *Come Back Mrs Noah* (1978), *Oh Happy Band* (1980), *'Allo 'Allo* (1982-92), and the *Are You Being Served?* spin-off: *Grace and Favour* (1992-93).

Are You Being Served? was nominated for a BAFTA in 1977 for Best Situation Comedy and *The Return of 'Allo 'Allo* won the RTS award for Best Network Entertainment Programme in 2007. For more information go to www.davidcroft.co.uk

ABOUT THE ADAPTERS

David Pibworth, David Lovesy and Steve Clark have worked together on a wide range of writing and theatrical projects through Milton Keynes Theatre of Comedy. They have developed stage adaptations of *Ripping Yarns*, *Porridge*, *Vicar of Dibley*, *Steptoe and Son* and *Hancock*, as well as pantomimes and murder mysteries. The trio have also performed in several runs of the original *'Allo 'Allo* play script and are delighted to provide performers and audiences with this sequel – meaning groups everywhere no longer have to 'stage this only wurnce!'

www.ingramcontent.com/pod-product-compliance
Ingram Content Group UK Ltd.
Pitfield, Milton Keynes, MK11 3LW, UK
UKHW021839210426
5322IPUK00022B/373